More Than Enough

Praise for *More Than Enough*

Few things inspire my weary heart more than the testimonies of women who have encountered Jesus in their own weary seasons. We're told in John's Revelation that the blood of the Lamb and the testimony of His saints are the two secret ingredients we need to overcome adversity! Perhaps you've known the cleansing flow of Christ's blood, but you still struggle to break free from the chains that bind you, the fears that plague you, and the self-doubt that keeps you small and silent. These women share their stories and testimonies, of the bondage-breaking power of God at work in a woman's life! It's time to overcome!

Wendy Speake, author of *The 40-Day Sugar Fast,*
The 40-Day Feast, and other books

Man gives titles. God gifts assignments. Because you're precious in His sight, He sees you . . . El Roi. In *More Than Enough,* you're going to feel seen by the God who wove every fabric of your being, while also being encouraged that you're already enough, right where you are.

Lisa Lou, founder of Lisa Lou Fitness, *Age in Reverse* Podcast,
health, life, and wellness coach, Faith Forward Age Backward
(F.F.A.B.) Energy Transformation

More Than Enough reminds us of the good news that produces great joy of our identity and authority in Christ! You have been called and chosen for such a time as this and no matter what you have been through in life, God reminds us He truly works together all things for good for those who love him and are called according to His purpose. As you read these inspiring testimonies of ordinary women who said yes to Jesus, may you be empowered to rise up, stand firm, and walk boldly in all that God has for you—a fulfilling intimate relationship with Him and a call to impact the world for His glory and others' good!

Ashley Weston, founder of Hidden Truth Jewelry

More Than Enough: A Woman's Devotional is an absolute must-have for women of all ages. This devotional is a beacon of empowerment, guiding women to break free from societal constraints and find their true worth in Christ. With magnetic energy and the devotional's life-transforming principles, Tamra and the collection of authors have crafted a masterpiece that promises to uplift and inspire women on their journey to lasting fulfillment.

Krystal Parker, president, of the US Christian Chamber of Commerce

This is a cohort of incredible women of faith who are active in ensuring that women of all ages and backgrounds come to know Jesus in a more profound way. *More Than Enough* is intended to nurture women on their journey of "always becoming," walking in their true identity.

Alejandra Crisafulli, The Baller Coach, an award-winning master coach and global speaker with the 180 Method

More THAN Enough

The Silent Struggle of a Woman's Identity

A WOMAN'S DEVOTIONAL

Tamra Andress

NEW YORK

LONDON • NASHVILLE • MELBOURNE • VANCOUVER

More THAN Enough

The Secret Struggle of a Woman's Identity

© 2025 Tamra Andress

Published in New York, New York by F.I.T. in Faith Press, an Imprint of Morgan James Publishing. Morgan James is a trademark of Morgan James, LLC.

www.MorganJamesPublishing.com

Proudly distributed by Publishers Group West®

Morgan James BOGO™

A **FREE** ebook edition is available for you or a friend with the purchase of this print book.

CLEARLY SIGN YOUR NAME ABOVE

Instructions to claim your free ebook edition:
1. Visit MorganJamesBOGO.com
2. Sign your name CLEARLY in the space above
3. Complete the form and submit a photo of this entire page
4. You or your friend can download the ebook to your preferred device

ISBN 9781636984360 paperback
ISBN 9781636984377 ebook
Library of Congress Control Number:
2024933312

Cover Design by:
Rachel Lopez
www.r2cdesign.com

Interior Design by:
Chris Treccani
www.3dogcreative.net

Edited by:
Sharon Miles Frese

A portion of all book sales goes to support The Founder Collective, a non-profit serving as a mobilzed church to establish, disciple and catalyze marketplace ministers.

Published by F.I.T. in Faith Press

www.fitinfaithpress.com

THIS BOOK IS DEDICATED TO . . .

All the Esthers willing to speak up for the marginalized.

All the Deborahs sitting at the table with men and standing her ground.

All the Abigails who refuse to remain silent in the name of justice.

All the Ruth's who have fought and are still fighting
to break generational curses.

All the Hannahs who carry the heart of a mama
no matter their call, mission, or age.

All the Sarah's who remain steadfast in faith, patiently
waiting for the fulfillment of His promises.

All the Rahabs who undermined their value from an unspoken past that
left you empty and isolated and yet led you to Jesus.

All the Marthas running around making the most
of this precious life and homes.

All the Marys who have found rest in Him and still perhaps
struggle with an internal battle or past.

All the beautiful helpmates, the Ezer Kenegdos.

This book is dedicated to our sisters, our moms, our friends, our
daughters, the generations past, and the generations to come.

You are the warriors, and you're worth the fight and the written reminder
in this text.

May this book cement your identity and remind you
that you truly are more than enough.

He proved it on the cross.

Now, let's show up like it.

TABLE OF CONTENTS

FOREWORD
By Melissa Hughes

It is a privilege and honor to be writing the forward on behalf of Tamra and the women authors in this book. I met Tamra at a podcasting conference a few years back. I had been scrolling through the conference attendees' directory and read "Christian Business Coach" in the title of her business bio. I decided at that moment I had to meet her. She was the only one out of the entire group to be so bold about her faith at this secular event, and I knew she was someone I wanted to connect with!

I absolutely loved her energy and the joy that oozed out of her from the moment we started talking. I was so surprised to find out later that evening at dinner that there was more to her than her sparkly top, superstar business bio, and beautiful face. She had a story. Anyone who knows what a good story entails knows that it isn't only comprised of a rosy beginning and happy endings. Every good story has the valley—that time of testing, challenge, pain, heartache, struggle, and coming face to face with your deepest fears. We connected over sharing our stories.

There's a quote that I have used often in my story. And it is one that brought incredible freedom to my life during a season when my husband and I literally lived in a valley on a cemetery with our two small children while church planting in the heart of Wales, and it's this . . .

Mountain top experiences are for sights and inspiration,
but the fruit grows in the valleys.
~Billy Graham

I'm unsure where you're in your life right now or what caused you to pick up this book. But maybe you're finding yourself in a valley, perhaps not literally, like I was, but in your heart. I remember crying out to God, asking Him, "Is this your best for my life? There must be more!" What's interesting about the valley seasons of life is that you discover how "not enough" we really are. We discover our humanity, our insecurities, and our doubts and fears. We discover how limited we can feel at times, even when we're flexing the biggest faith muscle we've ever mustered up.

If you're there today, I get it. I've been there. But what was so liberating about that quote from Billy Graham was gaining the insight to know that what I was experiencing was actually a part of the process. My story wasn't a failure. It was a fortitude of character. It was a season of shedding—a letting go of striving and performance and the fear of not being good enough—all while discovering God's overwhelming love for me in my "not-enoughness." And that set me free. I learned that at the end of myself—God was there.

Right now, in our culture, we often only see the mountaintop experiences of people's lives. As a social media influencer and content marketing strategist, I see curated content all day long in my day job. It's so easy to judge a person's life by their shiny exterior, a photo they posted, or the

But the truth is, all of us are so much MORE than our highlight reel. We each have a story.

carefully crafted version of themselves that they feel comfortable sharing online. But the truth is, all of us are so much MORE than our highlight reel. We each have a story.

And like I said, a story isn't good unless there's a problem to overcome. What is a good story if there's no villain for the good guy to beat, crisis to avert, or quest to conquer? Imagine a story where the guy and girl meet, and they ride off into the sunset and live happily ever after.

B-O-R-I-N-G!

There is absolutely nothing interesting about that story. But isn't that the life we keep praying for? Or is that just me?

For the longest time, I thought following Jesus meant God would solve my problems. I mean, He literally introduced himself to me as a "savior," so it wouldn't be totally ridiculous to assume He's going to rescue me out of every negative experience. Right?

Wrong!

While we were living in the valley, I discovered this truth about myself and God (always a good combination). God doesn't want me to live as a beggar for a bailout regarding the problems I experience in life. He wants to mold me into a victorious builder of His kingdom. And that is going to require overcoming some battles in order to see the victory. It's understanding that our valleys don't derail us from our purpose; they enrich it. I

It's about becoming the person God has created us to be in its fulness for His glory.

would even go further to say our purpose isn't always the thing. It's about becoming the person God has created us to be in its fullness for His glory.

In fact, if you know Tamra at all, she often says, "We're always becoming." Our life is an evolution, not a destination.

There is as much purpose in the valley as in the mountaintop. But in a culture that only wants to celebrate the wins, successes, titles, and labels, we are being robbed of hearing about the battle it took to get there and the person we had to become in order to achieve the victory. We are missing out on a really good story.

And so I think this has been my desire as a follower of Jesus, a wife, a mother, a TikTok Influencer, a podcaster, a speaker, an author, and an entrepreneur (all the titles)—the desire to be more than the sum total of my highlight reel. Each of us has this desire, and it's to truly be seen for who we really are—the good, the bad, and the ugly. We desire to be known fully.

I love Hagar's story in the Bible. In Genesis 16, Hagar is introduced as an Egyptian slave woman who belonged to Abram's wife, Sarai. When Hagar was sexually and verbally abused by Sarai and Abram, she fled to the wilderness. While she was there, she cried out to God in her distress.

Have you ever found yourself in a situation that was so unimaginable or painful that the only thing you can think to do is cry out to God for an answer? Well, what she discovers in that moment is something so profound and beautiful. As God answered her, Hagar's response was this: "I have now seen the One who sees me" (Genesis 16:13).

She discovered that God saw her! He saw her fully. He knew the pain of her past and the promise she dreamed of. And when we catch the revelation that God sees us fully, we are no longer bound to success because we discover our significance.

What gets me excited about this book is that it's a compilation of women sharing their stories—stories that attest to women who have discovered that they are more than their struggle; they are significant. They are more than whatever label the world has put on them. They are more than what the church has put on them! They are more than the labels they have put on themselves. In a time when we must encapsulate our identity to the world in eighty characters or less on our Instagram bios, the women in this book are taking space to declare they are more than that by sharing with you their stories.

This book is a banner of freedom for women. This book is a stake in the ground for women to embrace all of who they are and who God has commissioned them to be. This book will release that to you, too!

That night, when Tamra and I met, we talked about how amazing it was that God had a way of turning our biggest messes into our most profound messages. Since then, I have personally witnessed Tamra call forth women and help them share their stories with the world because it is through our stories we discover this one thing: all of us are more than what you see right now. We aren't defined by our past if we don't want to be. We aren't defined by the labels the world might put on us. We haven't reached our destination because there's always this evolution of who we're destined to become.

As you go through the pages of this book and hear the stories of these women, I pray that you will see God as the author and perfecter of your faith! And wherever you are in your story, whether on the mountaintop, in the valley, or journeying through the landscape of your daily life—God is writing your story, and it's significant.

You are significant.

Melissa Hughes is a TikTok influencer, international speaker, and best-selling author. She has been booked twice on *The Kelly Clarkson Show* and featured for the *New York Times* best-seller *Primal Scream* on NBC. She has over 255,000 followers on TikTok, with over eleven million likes. She is also a best-selling author of *She Can Laugh* and a children's book titled, *Mommy Loves You When.* She has been involved in missionary work in the UK for several years with her husband and two children.

INTRODUCTION

By Tamra Andress

I've stood in a room full of people and felt completely invisible.
I've stood in the mirror fully naked and felt utterly worthless.
I've stood at the altar with hundreds of witnesses watching me vow to
a love I couldn't yet comprehend or receive.
I've stood in a room trying to silence the sound of my crying babies.

All of these standing moments pale in comparison to the moment I fell into a fetal position as the waves of memories from my past flooded me after decades of suppression. And it wasn't the stale, lifeless, sing-song tunes or religion that picked me up . . . it was Jesus.

Thank God.

We've all been there—each and every one of us. Whether you can name the exact moment or emotion, you can point out, in essence, where your body holds the pain and where your heart carries the compassion. We are linked, both as Eves and as Esthers.

There is a rhythmic beauty to our connected power as women. Nothing can stand against it, and all of us must stand up for it.

We are women.
We are female.
We are ezers.
We are wisdom.

And while we may not carry the torch to our tombstone with these titles—this is our totality—regardless of how society tries to twist, turn, abuse, or taunt this fundamental, eternal truth.

In the beginning, God created. He said, "Let us make mankind in *our* image [yes, *our*... Father, Son, and Holy Spirit. Jesus was there at the beginning too], in *our* likeness, so that they may rule over the fish in the sea, the birds in the sky, the livestock and all the wild animals, and all the creatures that move along the ground. So God created mankind in his own image, in the image of God he created them; male and female he created them" (Genesis 1:26–27, emphasis added). And He called *us* very good (Genesis 1:31). And therefore no weapon formed against us shall prosper (Isaiah 54:17) . . . even if we become our own weapon (which is most often the case).

We were created and formed in our mother's womb to prosper, while humanity, in its choice of sin, births us into that very thing—sin. Our identity at birth starts to be mutated almost immediately upon our first breath. The world starts to speak of death, even at the inception of life. It starts to call us names, give us labels, and place us into categories and sectors of society based on external and internal forces we had no control over. In all areas—generationally, societally, politically, economically, emotionally, educationally, relationally, and spiritually—we are marginalized away from our true makeup. And eventually, those identities become our realities.

We become our bodies.
We become our titles.
We become our jobs.
We become our traumas.
We become our triumphs.
We become our family.
We become our faith if we're so lucky.

But, ultimately, we are more than those subsets of personhood.

We are not a pie chart of percentages. Like the Holy Trinity, we have three parts: soul (inclusive of our mind, will, and emotions), body, and spirit. And just as there is no finite line between the three persons of the Trinity, it is the same for us (even though our spirit has an eternal connection, while our soul and body are limited to this fleshly realm).

We are not a hat to wear or a ball to be juggled depending on the season of life, time of day, or day of the week.

We are not the lie that says we *choose* to be women. We were born as such.

And therefore, we are more than enough, just as we are—fully intended to be and to become.

And when we start operating in the fullness and wholeness of our aligned nature rather than in our secular, push-and-pull, heavy-laden yoke, we begin to operate in unforced rhythms of grace that breathe fresh life and bear much fruit.

I've been starving, and I've been full to the brim. And if you're reading this, I imagine you may have felt instances of both, too. The intention of this read is that you grasp hold of the bounty, overflowing with the living water, instead of the worldly, plastic, Barbie-infused culture that would love nothing more than for you to fit in rather than to stand out.

We are more than enough, just as we are—fully intended to be and to become.

As you read the stories of these women's uncovered testimonial truths (despite their momentary realities), you will be reminded that we are but sojourners here on Earth (1 Peter 2:11), and we must abstain from the passions of the flesh that wage war on our souls. We must come into our rightful inheritance as children of God, daughters of the Most High, crowned priests and kings (Revelation 1:5–6), and, ultimately, commissioned messengers of the gospel of Jesus Christ.

These devotionals are meant to be a light in the dark. They are meant to breathe hope and healing over the wounds of the world that we, as women, often carry as shame. They are meant to be connection points from her to you and you to her—from me to you and you to me. Ultimately, this leads us all to the Him that is within, as we are His image bearers (Colossians 3:10).

I pray that you see yourself in these stories, stories that you may have never fully lived, so that you can see Jesus in the midst and carry His ultimate compassion into every conversation, corner, and caveat you are bound to face here in this life. This life is promised to have trials and tribulations. But fear not, sweet woman of God, He has come to overcome, and we are already victorious in His name because of the blood of His son.

> *So I brush off my knees, and I stand once again.*
> *But this time . . .*
> *Not as a wife,*
> *Not as a mom,*
> *Not as a religion,*
> *Not as my body,*
> *Not as my job,*
> *And not even as my past.*

I stand as your sister. I stand as your friend.

In some sense, we are both of these and *more* or, as I like to say, "We are both/and." We are wives and mothers. We are spiritual beings and bodies. We are called and purposed, and we carry gifts and talents meant to be poured out to serve the kingdom mightily. He will use all things in our past for good. And He will dress us in dignity and strength as we laugh without fear of the future (Proverbs 31:25, NLT).

So, while our heart isn't to challenge you—you've been through enough challenges at this point—it is to call you to the front lines. To fight for *all* women. Fun fact: the Hebrew meaning for the word *all* is **all**. So no exclusions here!

In His strength and courage, will you make a stand with us?

Because together, we stand as a reminder—your reminder—that she can stand, too.

And He will get the final say. No matter what "they" say.

More THAN a Mom

"The father interrupted and said,
'Son, you're home now!' Turning to his
servants, the father said, 'Quick, bring me the
best robe, my very own robe, and I will place
it on his shoulders. Bring the ring, the seal
of sonship, and I will put it on his finger.
And bring out the best shoes you can find
for my son. Let's prepare a great feast and
celebrate. For my beloved son once was dead,
but now he's alive! Once he was lost, but now
he is found!' And everyone celebrated with
overflowing joy."

~Luke 15:21–24, TPT

CHAPTER 1

Rescued, Redeemed, Restored

By Heather Demorest

Life is made of many precious moments—moments of joy, excitement, peace, and happiness—moments that you wish you could hold on to forever. Other moments are filled with sadness, bitterness, regret, and grief. Often, we don't realize the value of a moment until it's passed. And sometimes, we don't realize the value of a moment until we lose the opportunity to create new ones. This is where my heart lingered on that hot Saturday in June 2023. I sat in a pew at the front of a tiny family church, staring at a photograph. The photo was of a beautiful, healthy young woman with a smile that lit up the room. She had a network of friends who were like family, an incredible job, and money to spend. When that photo was taken, she was living her best life, independent and free. Next to the picture sat a silver urn with purple roses etched throughout. She loved purple and flowers, so it was a perfect choice. My mind raced from thought to thought. . . . How are we here? How did this happen so quickly? My heart was drowning in a sea of grief, with a tide that was rising quickly. And at the same time, I felt numb. On that day, I was supposed to be 1,500 miles away for a conference where I would speak briefly about a chapter I had written for an anthology. I was not supposed to be here in this tiny church, sitting in a pew flanked by my brother and stepfather, minutes away from delivering the eulogy for my mom. It didn't seem real. The only thing my heart clung to was knowing that she passed peacefully, surrounded by her family. I felt such gratitude for the blessing of holding her hand when she took her last breath. I felt gratitude that I would get to celebrate her life, even though it was not something I wanted to do. My heart longed to talk to her.

Five years ago, I would never have imagined this moment—not of the passing of my mother but of the circumstances that would surround the end of her life. To be quite honest, I never really thought about it much at all and was indifferent about being there for her. As she aged, she struggled with health issues and had been declining for several years. In 2017, my grandmother passed away from dementia. It was the utmost honor to care for her while she was home in hospice. In her final days, I bathed her, sang to her, swabbed her mouth, and sat by her side. She was more like my mom than my mother. Grandma was my primary caregiver from the time I was an infant. She was the picture of love and care. She loved Jesus and her family more than anything. I would have done anything for her.

My mother, on the other hand, let's just say my relationship with her was complicated. So let me share a little background—that photo of the woman I mentioned was my mom in her prime—living in Dallas, dating a musician, and living her best life. She would become pregnant unexpectedly. Her boyfriend would ask her to have an abortion. Conflicted, she would move hundreds of miles away to live with her parents, leaving behind the life and friends she loved.

She gave birth to me in February 1978, thus marking the beginning of a complicated relationship. She nearly died during childbirth, and not long after, she returned to Dallas, leaving me with my grandma. My grandma used to tell me that when I started talking at about five months old, she called my mom and told her she needed to come home. . . . I was calling Grandma "Mama." From then on, we would ride the waves of her struggles, and there were many.

She struggled emotionally, mentally, and spiritually. As a child, I never really understood why. Through my eyes, I would see her pack up and leave town in the middle of the night. I would be shuffled to live with my grandparents, and my brother would live with Dad. I remember times she attempted suicide and struggled with alcohol and substance abuse. There were times she was so verbally mean to me that I would completely shut her out and call my grandpa for a rescue. This started when I was only three! My biggest fear was living *with* her. She was not safe or stable in my eyes. At times, I felt hatred for her. During high school, I cycled through living with several family members to avoid being in her presence after she told me, "If you want to be a little brat (PG version), that's fine, but don't come back here making my life miserable."

Our relationship became further strained when I married and had kids. I resented her attempts at advice. What did she know about parenting? She was a part-time mom, at best. I avoided her calls and avoided seeing her at any cost. I said terrible things about her. There was so much anger, resentment, and bitterness in my heart. I felt abandoned and not wanted. I became a people pleaser, and my identity was stuffed into the deepest, darkest corners of my soul. My relationship with her became only superficial. But God . . .

In 2021, God took hold of my heart. He began to transform me from the inside out. I would take her calls, but there were still destructive feelings. Her health was declining, and she was hospitalized more frequently. She didn't take care of herself, and I didn't want to hear about how she avoided her doctor's appointments. I didn't want to hear about the struggles she seemed to bring on herself. In my mind, she did not deserve a mother-daughter relationship with me. She would beg me to visit and spend time with her, and I would always make excuses about why I couldn't. I felt a resistance in my soul. "Why should I allow her access to me?" Little did I know this would soon change.

That fall, my family and I were in a transition period during a move. The move-in date for our new home was pushed back two weeks from the move-out date of our previous home. It was over the Christmas holiday in 2021. We packed up our life in a storage unit—along with every excuse I had not to make the time for a visit. We stayed at her house for two whole weeks. She and I spent the evenings talking, laughing, and watching our favorite movies. She was bed-bound, so I helped take care of her.

One evening, we were watching *The Wizard of Oz*. We talked about my childhood, and I shared with her a chapter I had written for an upcoming book. Finally, I expressed my feelings of being abandoned and unwanted as a child and how deeply hurt I felt by things she had done over the years. We also talked about how many of my actions had also caused her deep hurt. We both cried. We both hugged each other. Something beautiful and supernatural was happening. There was love, empathy, compassion, and forgiveness. There was finally peace. At that moment, God redeemed the years of our relationship that were stolen by anger, frustration, and bitterness.

> **Something beautiful and supernatural was happening. There was love, empathy, compassion, and forgiveness. There was finally peace.**

When I reflect on our relationship, I'm reminded of the parable of the prodigal son (Luke 15:11–24). In this story, the son decides to take his inheritance and go off to live his best life. After a while, the house of cards he built on reckless living began to fall. There was famine. He was financially destitute and unfulfilled, working as a pig hand. Life suddenly wasn't so great. He had a time of reflection and decided to return home. I can imagine what the prodigal might have been thinking. "Will he let me come home? Will he still love me?" As soon as the father saw his son in the distance, he began to run to him and met him with love and an embrace—no judgment or condemnation. A celebration followed. He was lost but had been found.

In my relationship with my mom, I've come to realize we were both prodigals in our story. Both of us had, at some point, left our relationship to pursue something better. She always left town for what was familiar and comfortable, where she lived her best life before becoming a mom, nurse, and wife. I avoided interaction, seeking safety and security elsewhere. Once I was an adult, I was determined to show her I would be the mother she never could be.

The time she and I spent together during those two weeks was priceless—moments I will hold on to forever. We were able to embrace each other with celebration. Our relationship was changed in miraculous ways. The past faded into the past. We agreed to live for the future. And over the next few months, Mom found a renewed relationship with God. She had a faith that I had never seen before and was relying on God each day. She became not only my mom but my best friend, confidant, and someone I sought out for advice. She would minister to me. I shared my biggest dreams and ideas, and she was one of my biggest cheerleaders. I visited often, and we both thanked God for our relationship that had been redeemed and restored. Back on that hot day in June, I stepped up to the microphone and delivered the most important message of my life. I recounted my mom's life for our friends and family. My only goal was to honor her for all the good—for all she overcame, for all she created, and for the impact she made. As I spoke of her life, my heart swelled with joy, and though I grieved her loss, I was so grateful I was her daughter for forty-five years— despite the struggles. And I was so thankful for the many golden moments she occupies in my heart, like her stories of putting herself through nursing school by waiting tables when I was a baby, making me chicken soup when I was sick with chickenpox, and taking me on Disney vacations that I will never forget.

So many memories flooded back. I remember the Nancy Drew books she gave me each Christmas with a personal note inside the cover. And when my oldest daughter was born, she loved and cared for her so tenderly—she was the proudest grandma. When I was in nursing school, she spent many nights on the phone with me, reviewing information and talking to me through disease processes. And she kept my seashells from our trip to the beach in 1986. . . . The good of her life outweighed the bad.

For the service, I selected a song I found more than fitting: "Through All of It" by Colton Dixon. The lyrics capture the essence of what life's journey is for most of us, as well as the myriad of feelings we experience. Sometimes we get it right; sometimes we don't. Through the journey, *God* is with us. He's there, even if we don't feel Him. What a blessing and honor it was to deliver the message to honor her life . . . to honor the legacy she left behind.

Mom lived a tough life, a broken life, not unlike so many others. But God brought the pieces of her brokenness back together like a masterpiece. He brought our broken relationship back together and sealed the cracks with gold! Mom was so many things to many people—wife, daughter, aunt, nurse, friend, colleague, and so much more. I am grateful and blessed she was my mom, but she was so much more than that. She was God's child—created with purpose on purpose. And by the grace of God, our relationship was rescued, redeemed, and restored.

My life would have been full of regret. But thanks to the power of our Lord and Savior, there is no regret.

My grandmother once told me that I should forgive my mom. She assured me that if something happened to her and I hadn't forgiven her, I would regret it. She was incredibly wise. My life would have been full of regret. But thanks to the power of our Lord and Savior, there is no regret. Sweet friends, if you are walking through a difficult relationship with your mom, I see you. I was you. Death was not powerful enough to keep Jesus in the grave, and it is not powerful enough to keep you from seeing redemption and resurrection in your relationship. Extend grace. Have a heart of compassion. Meet them with empathy. Allow God to work.

REFLECTIONS:

1. What actions from the past have led to broken relationships? How did this make you feel?
2. How does God's Word refute those negative feelings and thoughts? Spend time in prayer, asking God to release the negative emotions and thoughts attached to your relationship.
3. What is one step you can take today to start the healing process?

Heather Demorest is a Christian, wife, mom, business owner, life coach, public speaker, and two-time best-selling author! She is the founder of the "Living Aligned" group on Facebook, where she provides motivation to her followers! After stepping away from a six-figure corporate income, Heather now finds purpose and joy in helping others break the employee mindset, step into their God-given purpose, and pursue their God-sized dreams. She provides encouragement and support and shares the love of God through her presence on social media, her writing, and her speaking engagements.

"Being confident of this, that he who began a good work in you will carry it on to completion until the day of Christ Jesus."

~Philippians 1:6

CHAPTER 2

Transformed through Trust

By Robin Gulley

Hey, Mama, repeat after me! "I am a mother. My love is deep, wide, and knows no bounds. I believe, by the grace of God, my children will rise up and call me blessed. I will leave a legacy of faith in God, hope in His promises, and love of God. I am a mother—yet so much more."

Merriam-Webster Dictionary (Merriam-Webster, Incorporated 2023) defines a *mother* as a female parent. Children often call their mothers *mom*, an informal word for mother. But regardless of which word you use, if you're a mother, you know we're so much more than "a female parent." In fact, Proverbs 31:15–31 provides a myriad of otherness about females/ women and their motherly care for their households. If you've not read these verses before (and even if you have), read them now and consider the wonder of being created with the capacity to be all God created you to be. I'll be here when you return. . . .

I hope you found encouragement in the words of Proverbs 31, even if, like me, you've been challenged. Let's press into the challenge and be built up in our God-given capacity.

Our anchor verse, Philippians 1:6, has been my lifeline throughout much of my life, especially as I endeavored to raise and shape my children to be Christ-followers. Please reread the verse and allow it to ruminate in your spirit as I take you on a journey with me, a journey of the soul and spirit, a journey only God could have allowed and kept me through.

Travel with me back to the early years of my parenting and be encouraged to trust the God of the universe, His providential care and sovereignty, and His grace and mercy. I pray as we journey, you'll see He has entrusted you with the most meaningful work—bringing up your children to know Him—and that He has even more for you.

The year was 1985, and I was pregnant with my first child. The timing wasn't great, but it couldn't have been better. My father was battling lung cancer (he'd been given six months to live), and two of my three sisters were also pregnant. Our pregnancies seemed to give my father the stamina to live a little longer, and I was hopeful he'd meet my firstborn. And as is God's way, He allowed my father to live until my daughter was born. Six weeks later, the good work God had for my father came to its conclusion, and he transitioned to his eternal, heavenly home.

Before long, I gave birth to my second child, my son, and his middle name would be my father's first name—Samuel. He required more of me than I could have imagined. When he was three years of age, his father and I separated, and shortly after, we divorced. It didn't take long before we saw the effects this separation had on our son. He became angry and displayed frustration through behaviors that caused difficulties at home and school.

An incident occurred a few years later that rocked our world. At eight years of age, my son threatened to take his own life by grabbing a knife and aiming it at his abdomen. My daughter quickly gained control of the knife as I ran toward them, calling 911 on my phone. The police arrived shortly after the call and assisted in transporting us to a local mental health facility. My son was placed on a seventy-two-hour hold that would be extended for an entire week and one day—eight long days.

During my son's hospital stay, the Lord met me in ways I could have never imagined. I was working full-time at that time and still had to care for my daughter. Each morning of that week, I'd rise from bed and get dressed, take my daughter to school, get to work, and manage to walk into the office with a smile on my face. My coworkers questioned how I could smile while my son was hospitalized. I would have wondered as well had

God not met me as I cried out for Him to send the Comforter. The God of heaven and Earth heard my cry and left His throne to comfort me.

The Comforter came! He held me close to the bosom of the Father and reminded me of who I was in Him. He caught every one of my tears and assured me none were wasted. The

The Comforter gave me strength to gird up and then sent a sister to walk with me and encourage me in His Word.

Comforter gave me strength to gird up and then sent a sister to walk with me and encourage me in His Word. This sister shared a Scripture with me that would give voice to my hurting heart, and I began to read and recite it each day.

> *"Give ear to my words, O Lord, consider my sighing. Listen to my cry for help, my King and my God, for to you I pray. In the morning, O Lord, you hear my voice; in the morning, I lay my requests before you and wait in expectation."*
> **~Psalm 5:1–3, *The Women's Devotional Bible 2*, 1995**

The eight days came to an end, and my son returned home! The doctor at the mental health facility recommended we begin a medication that would help balance my son's brain chemistry. I'm not big on pharmaceuticals, so I researched (to learn more about the possible side effects) and prayed. After much prayer and feeling confirmed in my spirit, I declined the medication but knew we would need some sort of intervention and support.

I'd heard of a well-resourced Christian organization and reached out to learn what might be available to us. I was directed to a counseling facility that could provide a clinical assessment as well as individual and family counseling sessions. And the next phase of our journey began.

We traveled to the facility each week to complete questionnaires, engage in play therapy, and receive counsel. This was done in phases with one-on-one psychological assessment sessions for my son, which would include play therapy time, while my daughter and I would receive one-on-one talk therapy. We then progressed to family sessions, where we'd play a game together. And though the therapist played as well, he used the time to observe our interactions. As you might imagine, some sessions were better than others. Some weeks, my daughter openly displayed her displeasure with the amount of attention focused on her brother by taunting him. In other weeks, the taunting was mutual. Every week, I left sessions exhausted—exhausted but hopeful.

My children had vastly different needs. My daughter was independent and often behaved in a mature fashion, so it was easy for me to assume she was OK and didn't need much support or reinforcement. My son was dependent and frequently asked, "Right, Mom?" after sharing his thoughts on something—a request for validation. My daughter was responsive to my requests, but my son . . . not so much. This was indicative of the diagnosis we'd received—oppositional defiant disorder (ODD).

This diagnosis rattled me, but I knew I'd have to trust God with whatever this would mean for my son and our family. I developed a game plan—better behavioral boundaries and no small victories. Rest assured, I was put to task. This was not going to be a walk in the park. In fact, it would become exponentially more difficult with my decision to remarry. Our marriage would bring together two families—mine and his. We each brought to our union a daughter and a son. We were now a non-nuclear family of six.

It became my goal to graft my husband's children into my heart and make them as much as part of me as the children I birthed.

As you might imagine, these would be the dying years—dying to self—over and over and over again. And isn't that just the way it is when we decide to walk out of this life with a heart to honor Christ? When we married, our boys were eight and nine years old, and our girls were ten and thirteen. And you've probably already guessed that the sibling rivalry was just a little more intense.

It became my goal to graft my husband's children into my heart and make them as much a part of me as the children I birthed. I wanted our relationship to be a reflection of the way God grafted me (a Gentile) into His family. I initially called them my stepchildren, but as I began to see them as a God-given addition, stepchildren morphed into children—*bonus children*. It's funny how life is—I'd always said I would grow up and have four children, two boys and two girls. I love how God honors our childhood desires.

When we married, I was working full-time, but it wasn't long before I sensed the Lord prodding me to resign from my job and be fully available to our four children. And so it was. I left the workforce and donned my full-time mom gear, which included a book or two. Have you read any Dr. James Dobson books? I picked up *Parenting Isn't for Cowards* and learned strategies for being a courageous parent and for raising responsible children.

Our children have distinctly different personalities, ranging from confident and socially comfortable to insecure and socially uncomfortable—outgoing to reserved. And though they managed to settle into a relationship with one another over time, they struggled with my husband and me being married to someone other than their biological parents. Despite all my efforts, despite all our efforts, the struggle to be received was and is real.

So, during the dying years, I learned to be intentional about listening to our children with an open heart and mind. I learned to apologize for my shortcomings and failures and to seek forgiveness. I learned to forgive myself and to allow God to bring healing to the broken and wounded places.

I also learned to trust God completely. I frequently refer to these long, difficult, and challenging seasons as the "hard trust." This is what Proverbs 3:5 calls me to, calls us to. Read it aloud and make it a declaration. Read it, exchanging *your* with *my*, and begin by saying *I*. The original verse says, "Trust in the Lord with all your heart and lean not on your own understanding." Here's how you might declare it: "I will trust in the Lord with all my heart, and I will not lean on my own understanding." Let's really trust God; He's for us.

Speaking of trust, can we talk about expectations—those expectations we have for our children? Earlier in this chapter, you read about my son's mental health diagnosis and a bit of how he was challenged. Yet, interestingly enough, the Lord spoke to me about his future when he was around seven or eight years old. I recall hearing the Lord say my son would be a preacher—a minister of God's Word. But my son's life choices didn't align with the picture I'd painted for how ministry should look. I was biased and influenced by our Western culture's depiction of what a minister of God's Word looks like, how and where the ministry would and should happen, and what behaviors were indicative of the man of God.

I expected to see what God spoke come to fruition in the early years. However, my son was prone to anger and depression. It seemed he was waylaid whenever he was on track to achieve a goal or even when he was just trying to survive day to day. However, I often heard him singing late into the night. I'll never forget him singing the lyrics to "In the Name of Jesus" and "I Cast All My Cares Upon You." And one Sunday service, he sang a solo of "The Solid Rock" by Ron Kenoly (albeit karaoke style). But life and its choices have a way of taking us off course if we're not careful. And when you're young, you're often not careful. And when you're the mama, you often question if you heard right.

But God! Today, my son is ministering God's goodness and grace amid homelessness. This is not what I expected and not what I hope continues. . . . But God! Our anchor verse is as much for our believing children as it is for us and every believer. "Being confident of this, that he who began a good work in you will carry it on to completion until the day of Christ Jesus" (Philippians 1:6). And now I know—I heard right!

Today, my son Brandon Samuel goes by voice_samuel on social media. The Lord has given him a different voice than I expected and an amazing ability to communicate through the written word. And God has granted this mama peace. And though I haven't written much about my other children, rest assured there were mom expectations that went unfulfilled—yet again—but God! He will fulfill His plan and purpose in their lives (not based on my expectations). Praise the name of the Lord!

This journey of motherhood has transformed me into a woman I don't always recognize (a woman I can't fully explain), but I'll give it a try. I mentioned previously that I came home to be a full-time mom to our children; however, I eventually entered the workforce again. This time, I would work part-time as an instructional assistant in special education. It would prove to be a perfect job, as it allowed me to be home when our children were home and at work when they were at school.

I was well respected in the workplace and given responsibilities beyond that of an instructional assistant. The teaching staff encouraged me to return to school for a teaching credential. So, I enrolled in a program with the University of La Verne and completed the coursework required to receive a bachelor of arts degree in liberal studies.

This didn't happen without a fight. In the midst of attending school, I accepted a teaching job at a charter school for grades seven through twelve and was brought on as a part-time dance teacher. I loved every minute of teaching dance to students hungry to learn this art form, yet it wouldn't be long before I was promoted to campus director. During that season, I taught dance, was responsible for oversight of the campus, worked long hours, attended school in the evening, and supported my teenage children at home. But, before too long, my body began to rebel, and I would end up on disability for a year.

This season of disability created a new longing, a longing for better health and direction. I wanted to optimize what I learned as a mother and teacher. So, after a year, I returned to work at the electric company, and three years later, I returned to work in education. This is when it all began to click. I received clarity of direction and enrolled in a graduate program at Azusa Pacific University, obtaining my master of arts degree in educational and clinical counseling. I was especially drawn to the clinical counseling focus. My role as mom required me to learn, explore, and research what psychology says about the human psyche, human behavior, and our human experience. I compared this information with what God says about who we are and how we're uniquely and beautifully created. At that moment, I realized how desperately I was needed in the realm of education.

God opened the door for me to work in education with a different focus, a focus on behavioral and mental health. I was offered a job as a behavioral health specialist with the Hawaii Department of Education on the island of Maui. This was another opportunity to trust Him and move forward in courage. I'd experienced many courageous moments as a mom, but now it was time to bravely pursue and respond to God's new leading.

After a year of work on Maui, I returned to work in Southern California as a therapeutic behavioral strategist. This work in education has aligned my gifting, desire, learning, and God-given talents in ways I would have never thought possible. I work with students who remind me of my children, and my heart is filled with compassion and a drive to help them and their families. God is a broad-stroke God.

God's broad stroke eventually led me to start a ministry and business called Robin's Nest and write a devotional, *Dancing to Freedom*. But this is not your standard devotional. It has accompanying videos that incorporate dance and movement. This idea was born from a dream God placed in my heart to gather women together and use dance to explore soul issues. This would be for the express purpose of gaining freedom and healing so that each of us would become the woman God intended us to be. This

God has used every bit of the blessing and challenge of motherhood for my good and His glory.

kind of woman changes the trajectory of her life and that of her household. This woman's soul is free to live fully alive in Christ. She is transformed, renewed, and continually "becoming." As I write this, Robin's Nest is "becoming" driven by the desire to nurture and see others flourish and soar.

God has used every bit of the blessing and challenge of motherhood for my good and His glory. If you let Him, God will transform you, too, mama. He will use all you've experienced as a mother to propel you toward your God-given destiny. You will not be who you thought you were. You will be more; I guarantee it.

Motherhood is an all-encompassing, beautifully joyous, and painful journey. It is the highest calling. And if you've been granted the honor of being a mom, what more could you want? Motherhood is enough! And yet, it prepares and requires us to be more.

My mother tells me that her mother would say, "When they're little, they walk on your feet, and when they're older, they walk on your heart." And God wastes nothing! God is in the business of transforming us into the image of His son and will use anything—our hurt feet, hurt hearts— to get our attention and draw us close. And you can be confident that He who began the good work in you will complete it (Philippians 1:6).

Hey, Mama, repeat after me, "I am a mom, yet so much more because God has made it so."

REFLECTIONS:

1. In what ways has God called you to trust Him with your child(ren)?
2. How is God using your role as a mom to inform who He's called you to be?
3. How has God used your role as a mom to shape what you do?

Robin Gulley is the founder and owner of Robin's Nest, a ministry and business that provides a safe space for women (and girls) to explore soul issues through dance and movement. Robin's Nest empowers women to live in the freedom of their God-given identity as together we uncover and release traumas and challenging life circumstances. Robin holds a master of arts degree in educational and clinical counseling from Azusa Pacific University and is employed as a therapeutic behavioral strategist in her local school district.

More THAN My Body

"Be alert and of sober mind. Your enemy, the devil, prowls around like a roaring lion, looking for someone to devour. Resist him, standing firm in the faith, because you know that the family of believers throughout the world is undergoing the same kind of sufferings. And the God of all grace, who called you to his eternal glory in Christ, after you have suffered a little while, will himself restore you and make you strong, firm, and steadfast."

~1 Peter 5:8-10

CHAPTER 3

He Met Me in My Surrender

By Gina Aubrey-Wertz

"As I lie trembling on the floor in the fetal position, I wonder how many more days, weeks, or months I will have to wake up and endure this battle. The exhaustion is building, and the blows to my raw nervous system are like doing battle with a bulldozer. It's almost more than I can bear. This mysterious "health crash" has me down twenty-five pounds now. I know I need to feed my body nutrients, but I'm terrified of the aftermath of trying to eat or drink even the smallest amounts. My world then consists of going from my bed to the floor, to the bathroom, and back to the floor. I try to work up the energy to do a couple of Epsom salt soaks in the bath to help detox whatever is ravaging my body. The sunlight that I used to love beaming through the window now hurts my skin. I live my days in darkness with all shades lowered to block the light and silence the outside noises, fearing they will cause another episode."

This was a journal entry from 2017 and a glimpse of how I lived most days for nearly a year. As I lay on the floor weeping for hours at times, I would cry out, "God, what is happening?!" All I heard back for weeks was, "Trust the process." I did all I knew to trust the process, but in that bedroom, I was in a war zone, and this battle was fierce and unlike anything I had ever experienced.

I was terrified to be alone, but I could hardly bear anyone else in the room. My husband had to move into the guest room for weeks. It was months before I could handle even fifteen minutes at the family dinner table. In my life before this health crash, big family dinners were a regular event at our home, full of laughter, bonfires, kids, and grandkids. Nothing brought me more joy than those nights. My daughter Jessica, who knows how to talk me through my health struggles, was in the midst of her own challenging time. She was under strict orders to stay home after a complicated delivery and a postpartum hemorrhage during the birth of my second grandchild. It was hard for both of us to not be there for each other. I ached in my bones with loneliness and despair.

When the house was quiet, and I was alone, I would pull my trembling body out of bed and move slowly through my home, worshiping through tears and declaring victory out loud in the name of Jesus! One verse I sang on repeat was from a song by Andre Crouch, "The Blood Will Never Lose Its Power." If you grew up in a gospel church, I know you can hear this song in your head right now—followed by a hallelujah! I realized my battle was not just with flesh and blood. It was in the spiritual world as well. The spiritual warfare over me was real, intense, and where my victory was rooted (Ephesians 6:12). It was time to armor up and call in my warriors!

I decided to set up my bedroom for battle. My daily tools included my Bible, multiple journals, colored markers, and three-by-five cards to write verses on and hang all around my house. When I was strong enough to handle the TV, I kept it on the Hillsong Channel 24/7. God used the various messages, worship songs, and stories in numerous powerful ways throughout my healing journey. Bobbi Houston, the then-co-global senior pastor of Hillsong Church, had a powerful impact on me. She became one of my best "girlfriends," though she didn't even know who I was.

In time, word spread to my circle of friends concerning my health, and let me tell you, I am forever grateful to have such beautiful warriors on my team, warriors who know how to call on the name of Jesus! Soups and gifts were left at my doorstep, and I started receiving daily texts filled with Scripture and prayers. My home, inside and out, was anointed with oil, and every inch was covered in prayer. Once I became a little stronger, a couple of friends would come over and hold me by the arms for support so I could walk outside in the sun. I would cry with every step while they sang worship songs and prayed over me. I wish I could list every one of their names, as they are forever etched in my heart with gratitude.

There is one that I must mention, as she was pivotal in saving my life—Cindy Rivera. I called her my mountain-hippie doctor, which she would humbly smile at while continuing to rub lavender and fermented juice on my tummy. She served me pine needle teas and herb baths, deep diving for answers on how to holistically eradicate H. pylori, E. coli, and other culprits that played a part in my illness. Cindy filled me with hope and encouragement and prayed prayers upon prayers over me. I honestly could write an entire book on how this precious friend of mine helped me—mind, body, and soul—every single day for months. I love you, sweet friend!

But even Cindy would remind me, "At the end of the day, Gina, it's just you and God." Yep, we can have support, love, and help, but when it came to the breath I breathed, it was just me and my Creator. So my cries of desperation that asked, "Why is this happening?" eventually turned into, "Father, help me to be still and trust in the process." I knew I had a long healing road ahead of me, but I began to find comfort in soaking in God's Word like never before and learning to pray the Scriptures. I've always talked to Jesus, but now our talks were closer and louder than I had ever experienced. There is a sweet communion opportunity with God in our darkest times that cannot be reached until we are at the end of ourselves. My journals are filled with Holy Spirit-driven messages and downloads God poured into my heart.

God gave me many unforgettable visions that aligned with each part of my healing journey. One night, like many others, I was absolutely miserable. All I could do was lay in the dark, crying and praying until my exhaustion took over, and I drifted to sleep. The following day, I awoke suddenly hearing the words, "1 Peter 5:8." Nothing like this had ever happened to me. And though I have always loved Jesus wholeheartedly, I was never good at learning and remembering Scripture, so I had no idea what 1 Peter 5:8 said. But I could not wait to find out! I rushed for my Bible, fumbled through the pages, and began to read. "Be alert and of sober mind. Your enemy, the devil, prowls around like a roaring lion looking for someone to devour" (1 Peter 5:8). This was precisely what I was living in real time! As I kept reading, there it was . . . verse 10. "And the God of all grace, who called you to his eternal glory in Christ, after you have suffered a little while, will himself restore you and make you strong, firm and steadfast" (1 Peter 5:10). Wow! Oh my goodness, I could hardly hold it together as buckets of tears poured down my cheeks and hope poured into my soul. Almighty God had spoken directly to me from His Word and had reminded me that "after you have suffered a little while," He would restore you. I kept reading that part repeatedly because it meant there would be an end to this suffering! This stirred up a fresh layer of fight in me to keep going. I went from feeling like I was dying daily to a promise directly from the heavens! My healing did not come overnight, however. It has been a rocky journey full of challenges, unknowns, and roller coasters—a journey that has lasted for four years and still keeps me on my toes. But I would not trade the process for anything.

Before my health crash, I lived a fast-paced, type-A-personality lifestyle. I was a successful, high-level entrepreneur and business owner. There was a lot of international travel, entertainment, events, and never-ending to-do lists. While successful, this lifestyle carried enormous physical and psychological burdens I tried to mitigate through a passion for living holistically. So, when my health crash happened, it was a surprise for many in my circle. "You can't supplement your way out of a stressful lifestyle" is a phrase you may have heard before. Well, I learned firsthand that this is a correct statement! I had the best tinctures, supplements, and greens for my adrenals, hormones, and immune system. My home was filled with organic foods, juices, non-toxic household products, and stacks of books on holistic living. My backyard contained an organic garden, and my calendar was filled with many self-care opportunities.

Ok, so now let me share where the breakdown happened . . . I had very high levels of stress, skipped meals, and ate on the run (when I did eat). I'd catch myself shallow breathing and tense at my desk for hours. Over the previous twenty years, I had been on a pursuit to prove to the world that I was a fighter and an overcomer of a myriad of adversities. One of the hardest of these was becoming a widow at age thirty-two—with two young children at home. I lost my high school sweetheart and the father of my children to a drunk driver. My eleven-year-old daughter was also hit by that drunk driver, and is my miracle, as the doctors told me she most likely would not survive the night. Less than two years later, I was diagnosed with Hodgkin's lymphoma. Honestly, I barely had the strength and willpower to walk through that battle, but I did. I felt like I couldn't catch my breath in life.

A short handful of years after enduring these uninvited storms, God blessed my family by bringing my current husband, Tim, into our lives. I felt like I could breathe again; I had hope. My then seven-year-old son would say he felt like his daddy handpicked Tim and sent him to us; I felt the same. It takes a man of immense character to be able to walk in another great man's shadow, knowing I would still grieve the loss of my first husband and my children would always grieve the loss of their father. When he married me, he married all of us, and he did so with all of his heart. A few years later, when we became pregnant with our daughter Abigail Elizabeth, we felt we were finally living "happily ever after." But seven and a half months into my pregnancy, I knew something wasn't right. At almost full term, the doctor's appointment confirmed that there was no longer a heartbeat. I was induced immediately. It was torture. There are no words to describe the anger and pain in my heart. This was a rough one, really rough. Without going into the whole story, I spent two days in the hospital going through labor and the delivery of our beautiful, tiny, stillborn baby. This did me in. . . . And although God's grace and mercy helped us, saying I was broken would be an understatement.

You see, my health crash resulted from the weight of a multitude of mountains I had been carrying for a long time. For years, I had managed to silently carry this brokenness with me into every area of my life. During this crash, however, my mind would drift for hours, sometimes into the storyline of my past, until I would get jolted back into the nauseousness of my painful reality by an onset of debilitating anxiety, uncontrollable shaking from head to toe, and horrible pain in my gut. I could fill chapters on the different challenges each day brought and endlessly share how God showed up in big and small beautiful ways. But I have one moment, a moment that changed my life forever, that I must share. Months into my healing journey, I was lying flat on my back in bed with lights dimmed and gentle worship music playing. It was one of those very rough days, one with few moments of peace, and I was utterly exhausted. As tears

Very clearly in my soul, I heard, "Do you trust me?

rolled down my face, I began a conversation with God. At this point, our talks were frequent, and we conversed back and forth as if my best friend were at my bedside. I had stopped asking God why, but He knew and read my heart. Very clearly in my soul, I heard, "Do you trust me?"

I answered, "Yes, I trust you!"

Then I heard it again. "Do you trust me?"

This happened several times, and my answer was the same until finally, I answered with, "God, I have shown you how I trust you; through all the adversity, I have trusted you, praised you, and loved you."

Then God spoke words I will never forget! "Gina, I know you are strong and courageous; you have proven that to me. I know you are steadfast; you have proven that to me. Gina, I know you are an overcomer of many things, but . . . you have not proven to me that you fully trust me."

(Pause & Silence)

No words could describe how these words felt deep in my soul. Something within me broke off the chains I had been hanging onto, chains that convinced me I had to stay in the shoes of a fighter for my entire life! My version of trusting God was to say the words and praise His goodness, but I continued to hold on tightly to the reins of my life so that I could steer clear of any potential threats I saw coming for my family and me. It was exhausting.

I had to learn to let go entirely, and I began to surrender fully, probably for the first time in my entire life! I did not know what trust and surrender felt like, and it was tough. Stillness and surrender do not come naturally to me. I had to become like a newborn and learn from the beginning. Sometimes, we need to allow ourselves to be like newborns, seeing only eight inches in front of us and trusting God one step at a time.

He met me in my surrender! The magic (miracle?) happened in the waiting. My four-year healing journey was by far the most challenging hardship I have ever walked through, but it was also the most precious gift God has ever blessed me with.

By the time you read this story, you will have been covered by countless prayers that I have been praying for you, knowing (even before you knew) that you would be reading this someday. Trust me, He will meet you in your surrender.

xoxo,
Gina

REFLECTIONS:

1. What are the mountains you have been carrying?
2. What shoes you have been walking in that God did not assign to you?
3. What do you need to surrender?

Gina Aubrey-Wertz has been a warrior and a survivor of many uninvited storms in her lifetime. She is finally following a dream God deposited in her heart many years ago of putting pen to paper and sharing pieces of her story of resiliency powered by God's grace! This first writing endeavor will share a riveting testimony of a healing journey that was both brutal and beautiful as God spoke to her soul in dark places and walked her through a three-year healing journey.

This is the first of many stories to be shared both on paper and in person from Gina as she walks into a new season of adding *Author* and *Speaker* to her entrepreneurial resume. She believes we are all called to leave a positive mark and share the love of Jesus with a bruised and tattered world.

"But he said to me, 'My grace is sufficient for you, for my power is made perfect in weakness.' Therefore I will boast all the more gladly about my weaknesses, so that Christ's power may rest on me. That is why, for Christ's sake, I delight in weaknesses, in insults, in hardships, in persecutions, in difficulties. For when I am weak, then I am strong."

~2 Corinthians 12:9-10

CHAPTER 4

My Intestine-mony

By Penelope Sampler

When I was twenty-five years old, I was diagnosed with Crohn's disease. It has been a long journey, but not a journey without hope. If I had known then what I know now, I would have avoided an incredible amount of pain and heartache for my family and me. I would have prevented thirteen painful abdominal surgeries. I wouldn't have missed weeks of work. I wouldn't have had to move back home twice to be nursed back to health. I wouldn't have spent nights sleeping on my bathroom floor or tucking my children in and then driving myself to the emergency room. I wouldn't have missed my boys' school programs because of tests and procedures or had my sweet children find me motionless in pain on the floor. My husband wouldn't have missed days of work, and I wouldn't have missed days of my life fighting through debilitating pain. I wouldn't have taken an enormous amount of medication or worried for the life and health of my third child as he grew inside of me. My husband, parents, and children wouldn't have had to worry . . . if I knew then what I know now.

However . . . If I knew then what I know now, I wouldn't have suffered nearly as much, but I also wouldn't have clung to my hope and faith in God. I wouldn't have found myself praying so desperately to be healed, and I wouldn't find myself here, writing about hope for those who suffer from Crohn's or any debilitating disease. Where would the miracle be in my story if I knew then what I know now?

Roughly thirty-three years after my first stomach pain, I stand in awe of how the Lord wove together every aspect of my life into a masterfully planned and miraculous story of healing from a chronic and debilitating disease. He used every piece of my life to write His story through

He used every piece of my life to write His story through me.

me. He opened my heart years ago to desire a true life purpose and to yearn for a personal testimony that would allow me to be used for His purposes. He molded my spirit into

one that fiercely desired to deepen my faith and knowledge of Christ. He ultimately taught me to surrender everything I had left in the darkest of hours to trust in His plan completely.

> *"For I know the plans I have for you, declares the Lord, plans to prosper you and not to harm you; plans to give you hope and a future."*
> **~Jeremiah 29:11**

The Spiritual Trifecta

By the time I was twenty-five, I had recovered from two emergency abdominal surgeries. Shortly after the second surgery, I met my husband. A year and a half later, we were married and were ultimately blessed with three healthy boys. But the Lord was just getting started with us. I was involved in a great Bible study that challenged me to find my purpose, but the thought of my life's purpose had never crossed my mind. I had three little boys, and I was struggling to make it one day at a time just being a mom and living with a painful illness.

My husband and I also joined a brand-new Sunday school class. Our class spent the first weeks sharing our testimonies with each other, which only fed my insecurities. I didn't have a testimony. I didn't even know when I became a Christian. I grew up in a strong Christian family and had always lived with a firm faith. My story was relatively dull, as was my testimony.

The third piece of this trifecta occurred when our minister challenged us to pray for trials in our lives. Struggles typically bring you to prayer and growth in your faith. We had no idea what was beyond those prayers, but our world was about to be rocked. We knew at the outset that we were praying to deepen our faith and trust in the Lord. We wanted to lean into His strength and not our own.

"Consider it pure joy, my brothers and sisters, whenever you face trials of many kinds, because you know that the testing of your faith produces perseverance. Let perseverance finish its work so that you may be mature and complete, not lacking anything."
~James 1:2–4

Over the next several years, we added many tools to our faith arsenal. My health was already in a sharp decline, and my husband ultimately left his job, his entire career, to work closer to home and be available to our family. Every change he made confirmed that the Lord was guiding his steps. God was putting him in a place that could support him when he needed it the most. The Lord was moving before us with a hedge of protection, yet we couldn't see what was coming.

My doctor's visits became more serious. Conversations were heavier, and my overall status was becoming more concerning. My stays in the hospital increased in frequency, and more difficult decisions arose with blood transfusions, new medications, painful procedures, and visits to multiple specialists. My determination to be normal was beginning to show cracks, as I could no longer hide my pain or show up consistently as a healthy mom.

"But those who suffer he delivers in their suffering; he speaks to them in their affliction."
~Job 36:15

Prayers Were Being Answered

I was accepted to the Mayo Clinic, and we knew this was the answer to all my problems. After having some discouraging discussions, I received a single positive report. I looked the very stoic doctor in the eye and said, "That is great news, isn't it?" He stared at me blankly, and I repeated myself. He half-smiled and said, "You have lots of room for improvement, but yes, I guess that's an improvement." He went on to tell me he believed that if I were on the Oregon Trail, I would have made it to Oregon without a doubt. He said to me that most people in my condition rolled into his office in a wheelchair, looking awful. He said I was a very sick girl, yet I looked nothing like the others.

One of my previous doctors told me he put me in the "NCS" category—the "Non-Complaining Souls." I never wanted to be a martyr or praised for being tough. I did have pain, a lot of it, but I also didn't want my disease to define me. If I complained every time I had pain, no one would want to be around me. I was in chronic pain. And at that point, my prayer posse had prayed for fifteen years for my healing. On days I was down, I thought, "Why can't I be that miracle? God can heal me, so why isn't He? Why do I have to go through this?" I remember asking my mom, "When will I get the chance to be healed?" I knew people were praying for me, and God could heal me if He wanted to. So why weren't my prayers being answered?

As my case worsened, I was referred to the University of Texas Medical Center in Houston, and the parade of residents began, each nonchalantly asking me what was wrong. When I detailed my surgical history and the extent of the pain I was in, one resident responded, "But you look so put together." I had already been through so much that week and didn't feel like proving my misery. As soon as she read my chart, she grimaced and told me what a sick girl I was. I already knew.

By the frequent shocked looks and the doctors' desire to share my case with the medical students every time I landed in the hospital, I knew I looked better than I should. I was so grateful for that and knew there was only one reason—I was covered in prayer by legions of amazing friends.

"Be joyful in hope, patient in affliction, faithful in prayer."
~Romans 12:12

I returned to my own doctor for an endoscopy. After I was prepped, he said to his nurse, "This one, she's a fighter!" While I appreciated his sentiments, I got lost in thought and wished I didn't have to be a fighter. I had visions of the Mayo doctor telling me I should be in a wheelchair and wondered what it looked like to stop fighting, to just climb in that wheelchair and simply give up. And for that brief moment, I exhaled with the relief that came with those thoughts . . . but only for that moment, thankfully snapping back into the reality of my wonderful life with my amazing family. Who wouldn't fight for this? It was hard to keep it all together at times, but wasn't that the lesson I was there to learn, to trust in the Lord and lean not on my own understanding, to acknowledge Him in all my ways? He was taking care of me. After years of standing before doctors as they looked at me in disbelief at the severity of my illness, it finally started to sink in that I really was a sick girl.

As I became more coherent following that endoscopy, I heard them say that my procedure was aborted—my stomach wasn't emptying. I started to cry. My kindhearted doctor knelt beside me and said he didn't know what to do next. For the first time in my life, I understood the glorious promises of my body being renewed in heaven. I dreamed of my earthly body being made perfect and without pain. I felt very intimately the deepest desire to be pain-free and to be whole again.

"Our bodies are buried in brokenness, but they will be raised in glory. They are buried in weakness, but they will be raised in strength."
~1 Corinthians 15:43, NLT

Discouragement filled my very being—discouragement for the years and years of prayer and faith that I *could* be healed while now facing the possibility that God would not heal my earthly body. But . . . I was beginning to see that God *was* answering my prayers. While I wasn't healing physically, I wasn't missing out on being a mom, wife, and friend. It was a miracle I was not in that wheelchair. It was a miracle that I had three beautiful boys amid fifteen years of a tough illness. It was a miracle that no one could tell by looking at me that I was sick. My prayers were already being answered.

God *was* healing me, but it was definitely not how I expected it to happen. There was no "you're healed" moment. However, the Lord was allowing my broken body to do things I shouldn't have been capable of doing. I was getting to live a full life despite the severity of a typically unforgiving illness. I was completely unaware of how those prayers were being answered in those years, but the fullness of my life was the answer. Those prayers were sustaining me.

But . . . if I hadn't struggled for so long, there would be no story to tell. I didn't know it yet, but I was the lead actress in the middle of an

I didn't know it yet, but I was the lead actress in the middle of an incredible storyline, with the most unexpected ending remaining to be seen.

incredible storyline, with the most unexpected ending remaining to be seen. The world was hearing the narrative. Friends, family, and strangers alike were praying so hard for me and experiencing the lows alongside me. Not only was the Lord teaching my family and me about faith and perseverance in prayer, but He was also teaching my prayer warriors, those who had been faithful in praying for me over not weeks or months but years.

My blog in December of 2014 revealed my renewed battle cry for my family and me: "I fight for my kids, and I fight for my family. I fight because I know God has bigger plans for me through my disease. I don't know what they are. I don't know when or how this story ends. But I know that somehow, God is working His purposes through me. I have never been weaker, but also know I have never been stronger."

I was never angry with God, as our pastor once inquired. I just wanted to be sure that the glory would be given to the Lord during this awful time. I didn't want to wallow in self-pity or lose sight of the ultimate purpose for which I was searching. I knew that I was sustained daily by His strength alone. We knew that God was working through us, and nothing was more exhilarating to me than to know that God knew *me* and was using *me* to do something for His kingdom. I still begged for healing. I still cried out, asking, "When is this over?" But, ultimately, God was in control. My husband and I had discussed the "what ifs." But all those fears were not ours to bear.

> *"For God gave us a spirit not of fear but of power*
> *and love and self-control."*
> **~2 Timothy 1:7, ESV**

I woke up on a Sunday morning in miserable pain. It was my husband's Sunday to work, so I used every bit of energy I could muster to get myself and the boys to church. I wanted so desperately to be worshiping in the sanctuary. Praise and worship music was a window to my soul. It filled every part of my body with unspeakable joy. I walked into that sanctuary nauseous and in pain, with three boys in tow. I was unsure if I would have to run to the restroom, so I prepared my oldest son to watch the other two if I did. As we stood for the first song, I started to cry.

My sweet oldest said, "Does it hurt that bad, Mommy?" which made me cry more.

I looked at him and smiled. "No, honey. I am crying because it doesn't hurt at all."

When we left, I called my husband to tell him I was without pain the entire time I was in that sanctuary. I had a spiritual experience that I had never had before. In that place, I felt like I was standing in the presence of God. The Holy Spirit was there, and I was surrounded. I was so emotional and so relieved to have even a moment without pain. As we walked to the car, my pain slowly crept back over my body, but it could not diminish my amazement at the temporary healing I had experienced by simply standing in worship—I wanted to stay there forever.

I had been fighting this battle for half my life, and I hated many things about it. I hated that people worried about me and the pain it caused my family. I hated not being able to eat at any given time and missing out on entire days when I couldn't function. I felt Satan's pull. But I knew that he wouldn't win. I was stubborn, and I refused to be taken down.

"I can do all things through Christ who strengthens me."
~Philippians 4:13, NKJV

My blog in April of 2015 revealed the continued severity of my condition and the tenacity of those who fought by my side: "Today, the doctor, for whom the University of Texas Medical GI Center is named, told my husband, 'She is a strong woman! Most patients in her condition are completely debilitated. She has a strong will.' Then he looked so compassionately at me, calling me his girlfriend. 'This is complicated,' he said. 'You are complicated. But don't you worry because we "do" complicated here. We can fix complicated. It is just going to take time.'"

I didn't feel strong at all. In fact, I felt pretty broken. I was not tough. And every day, my optimism and fight were diminishing. There was no way I had the power or the strength to endure the pain for much longer. And certainly not alone. I was surviving completely on the faith that I could be healed and the prayers that were sustaining me.

"Therefore we do not lose heart. Though outwardly we are wasting away, yet inwardly we are being renewed day by day."
~2 Corinthians 4:16

Soon after, I became severely septic following surgery to remove the majority of my stomach. I spent seven more weeks in the hospital with eight more excruciating surgeries. My frame was now fragile, having lost over forty pounds in only two months. But God showed up in ways that brought us to our knees. The text chains full of desperate pleas for prayer and healing for my failing body during some very dark days slowly shifted to one praise at a time. Discouraging reports from all of my doctors began to show incremental signs of improvement. Step by step, we gathered our miracles in our arms and held on tight as we watched and waited with expectancy for more. Total recovery from that final stage of healing and the restoration of my physical strength took about two years of patience, dedication, and hard work.

Healed

It has now been six years since my recovery from having the majority of my stomach removed and the sepsis that followed. My Crohn's is classified as "inactive," but I know I am healed. Few get to claim healing from such a brutal and painful disease. I know how blessed I am to be living the second half of my life without pain. God heard the thousands of prayers of the faithful who prayed on my behalf for many years. He created the most incredible testimony, one I never thought I would have, and when we prayed for challenges, He certainly delivered. I fought for twenty-one years, always believing I could be healed, knowing God could

My story is now the platform for which my life's purpose was divinely created.

heal me, and expecting God to heal me. Had I not endured for all those years, I wouldn't be who I am today. My illness never defined me. But the physical and emotional scars it left behind, in addition to the strengthening of my faith and relationships and the miracles we witnessed, created who I am today.

My story is now the platform for which my life's purpose was divinely created. I unashamedly share the healing mercies I received and the incredible miracle of prayer over twenty difficult years. My minister encouraged me to tell my story to all those who fervently prayed for me for so many years so that they, too, would know their prayers were heard. And I am thankful that my story stands as a witness to them for their faithfulness. I share God's power that I know was revealed through my weakness when I had no fight left inside of me. I knew I had absolutely nothing left to give.

Yet, I was consistently told of my strength. I was no hero, and I was far from strong; I was weak both physically and emotionally, and I was almost completely defeated outside of this spiritual strength that empowered me. The strength people witnessed was my God because His power was made perfect in my weakness. His power that rested on me sustained me. His power alone healed me. Praise the Lord!

> *"But he said to me, 'My grace is sufficient for you, for my power is made perfect in weakness.' Therefore I will boast all the more gladly about my weaknesses, so that Christ's power may rest on me. That is why, for Christ's sake, I delight in weaknesses, in insults, in hardships, in persecutions, in difficulties. For when I am weak, then I am strong."*
> **~2 Corinthians 12:9–10**

REFLECTIONS:

1. Do you know what your God-given purpose is in life?
2. Are you willing to pray for challenges in your life so that God may deepen your faith?
3. Have you ever been angry at God for a difficult or painful circumstance you have endured?

Penelope Sampler calls both Texas and Oklahoma home. She received her bachelor's degree from TCU in Fort Worth and her master's in occupational therapy from Washington University in St. Louis. She practiced OT in various clinical settings, including the NICU, orthopedics, traumatic brain injury, and skilled nursing. After being diagnosed with Crohn's disease, she moved into pharmaceutical sales. Having been trained in the medical model and treated with many medications and surgeries, Penelope slowly shifted into the world of natural remedies when those medications and surgeries failed her. Although skeptical at first, her health improved dramatically using plant-based medicine. She started her platform BecomingNatural.com to share her story of healing, faith, and a good sense of humor in order to help anyone battling a chronic or debilitating illness. In addition to being a licensed occupational therapist, Penelope is a certified cannabis/CBD coach and a certified leadership coach.

More THAN My Religion

"See what great love the Father has lavished on us, that we should be called children of God! And that is what we are! The reason the world does not know us is that it did not know him."

~1 John 3:1

CHAPTER 5

More Than a Religion—His Children

By Jenny Ingels

In a recent conversation with other Christians, we discussed church attendance. Half of those present recalled moments in their lives (while visiting or attending a church service) when another Christian tapped them on the shoulder, cleared their throat, or motioned for them to move because they were sitting in *their* seat. Just imagine . . . if Christians do this to one another in a house of worship, how much more do these behaviors harm the faith of others who have come to see but have not yet believed?

My first significant experience with religion as a little girl started with no expectations and left me with a handful of disappointments. I remember my first time at Bible study when I was asked about a picture of Jesus. I didn't say who He was but only that I knew Him personally, and the children laughed at me. I found myself relegated to the younger classroom, where I was discouraged from talking about my relationship with the Lord but encouraged to use my hands and recite the words, "This is the church, and here's the steeple, open it up, and see all the people." I wondered how all the people really fit under that one steeple and was certain that God was far greater and did not need us to build Him one. That young girl grew up surrounded by Christian religions that left her with more and more disappointments. She often felt empty (instead of filled with joy), lectured to (instead of conversed with), or left out (instead of included) and far from being close to the Lord.

But even when I could not find the Lord under those steeples, I continued to search for Him. I realized that He could be found in the wilderness of my life . . . those places where I face the unknown, the unfamiliar, and the uncertain . . . those times filled with difficulties, frustrations, and confusion. It is then that He calls me to trust in Him. And it is in those places where He reveals himself—a gentle breeze, a golden sunset, the details, and the big picture, the comfort of family, conversations with strangers, time spent with friends, in my best moments, and at my worst—and He provides the way through. God has answered my prayers and made himself known without help from others and despite human restrictions. Man-made religions have created traditions and expectations that leave people distant, joyless, and yearning for more. And many of God's children no longer seem to be clamoring to gather under one steeple.

I learned outside the church pews that God is capable of anything. He is kind, funny, generous, merciful, and wise. He is full of grace and jealous of our relationship with Him, a relationship that is significant, palatable, and real. He doesn't take it lightly, and neither should we. If you ever doubt His greatness, look around at His creation—you'll see Him everywhere. Glance up at the sky, and you'll have immense confirmation of His presence. So why do we try to contain Him? Why do we try to claim individual and collective ownership of Him? Why do we demand that our church's precepts are the right and only way to receive Him? Christ lived and died for our sins to reconcile us to our Father, but this relationship is personal and deserves more familiar attention than it is often given.

If you ever doubt His greatness, look around at His creation—you'll see Him everywhere.

Having had the honor of traveling the world and meeting people of different backgrounds, cultures, and traditions, I've pondered how vastly diverse we really are. And I've realized how crazy we must be to stake our little claims in corners of our world and make declarations to others that if they want salvation, they can only find it here—at this church, on this pew, and under these conditions. How destructive, exhausting, and truly disrespectful to God! I had a friend tell me that it was great that I had accepted Jesus as my Savior, but because I wasn't baptized, I was going to hell. Others have told me that their religion is the best and most direct path to heaven, so, therefore, my personal faith in Him and my intimate relationship with Him are not. I've also had Christians try to convert me to Christianity. They weren't listening or interested in hearing about my relationship with Him, just their personal ideas about religion. And while I did eventually get baptized, it was out of a physical reflection of the posture of my heart, not to meet some other man's religious ideals and expectations.

I pray for all the believers and non-believers who live in conflict. "Lord, help our confusion, our division, our wandering hearts. Please love us all, forgive us all, protect us all, heal us all, and for all who don't have prayers being said for them or know your greatness, may you see them and show yourself to them." Most of all, I find myself longing for the day when we get out of God's way and start serving from our relationships, not our religions.

In today's climate, believers tend to shrink back from the gospel of Jesus, selling short the value of the Savior and the greatness that He brings to our lives and to the world at large. We hide what freedom through salvation looks like from the broken world around us by behaving like people who aren't free and failing to declare His glory. Our presumptive judgment, vast opinions, and selfish ways keep getting in God's way. But when we are in a relationship (not religion), we kneel before Him out of respect and honor. We quit pushing our way to the front of the line and stop staking claims on the church pews as if we own them (or Him). We look around to see those searching for true freedom and point them to Him. We let others cut in line, encouraging them to go forward in pursuit of their Creator because He's awesome and He loves them. Believers of Christ know what it means and how amazing it is to be called His child, so we step outside our comfort zones and look for the lost and lonely. We meet them where they are—in the wilderness of their lives. We pick up the wounded and the broken-hearted and breathe new life into them through His encouraging words. We tell them they can be born again into a new life and a relationship that is waiting for them. We draw them closer to Him by offering His love, not our religions.

Recently, I dreamt of a bride preparing for her wedding. She was disheveled. Her shoes didn't work with the dress, the veil wasn't attached, and her makeup was a total mess. People were all around her, moving in different directions, chaotic, busy, but unhelpful. Frustrated and in a hurry, she dropped her jewelry. The ring she'd been holding broke, and stones fell out of their settings, scattering over the floor. I realized that her heart was divided—she was torn between the affairs of this world and the King who was on the way for her. Her priorities were misaligned, and her concerns were self-reflective and based on how she looked in the mirror rather than how blessed she was to be chosen as his bride. In the disorder, she ran about, oblivious and frustrated . . . until she stopped to pick up the pieces of the broken ring. It was then that she noticed that the setting was not the jeweler's original design. And at that moment, she heard an audible voice above the crowd that said, "Make your own way." Suddenly, she realized who she was—a bride unprepared for her King—and she knew it was up to her to change the course of the preparations.

We have more time to get this right, to return the church to its original setting, its original design—a gathering of His people, not buildings or business.

In interpreting this dream, it was clear that these wedding preparations represent the state of the modern church. The bride is the body of believers and the coming king or bridegroom—Christ. Thankfully, He is delayed. We have more time to get this right, to return the church to its original setting, its original design—a gathering of *His* people, not buildings or businesses. This wedding is personal to us, and we should all be concerned with the details. The bride should pause and recognize how blessed she is to receive Him. She then needs to remove all the disorder and distractions (sins and idols) that are interfering with her desire to put this marriage first. She should change her shoes (where we disciple), alter her dress (how we disciple), tidy up her look (how we behave), and collect those scattered gems (the people). God longs to help His bride prepare; why else would He have announced His arrival in advance? And we should be grateful that He didn't leave His bride without an attendant. He sent the Holy Spirit to help her. And, oh, how we need Him.

> *"But you will receive power when the Holy Spirit comes on you;*
> *and you will be my witnesses in Jerusalem, and in all Judea and*
> *Samaria, and to the ends of the earth."*
> **~Acts 1:8**

> *"Then the church throughout Judea, Galilee, and Samaria enjoyed*
> *a time of peace and was strengthened. Living in the fear of the Lord*
> *and encouraged by the Holy Spirit, it increased in numbers."*
> **~Acts 9:31**

These words remind us we're not finished yet. The Lord delays for a time so more can be invited. From heaven's throne, He whispers, "Go get my people."

Personally, I put this dream's interpretation to the test by starting with myself. I stripped down to a proverbial sackcloth and covered myself in past ashes. I implored God to reveal to me all my sins and idols. I asked for forgiveness and help to remove the rest. While at first inviting, it was also a bit frightening—self-exploration of our sinful nature always is. But by the time it was over, it had become enlightening. He wanted to use that which I had used to sin against Him for good. I prayed for His help and cleansing to be made new. This wasn't the first time, nor likely the last. But these things that I held on to, carted around with me, and stewed in were dragging me down, pulling me under, and keeping me out of a true relationship with Him. I also couldn't serve Him until I offered Him my heart. I needed these sins to be forgiven, and these idols melted down so I could get back up and move forward. I needed to lose myself in Him so I could find myself again. Lost in my transgressions, He took me through a storm. On the other side were two rainbows, where He doubled down on His promises and my portion.

With a joyous, grateful heart and a willing spirit, I inquired of Him, "Where do I begin?" In short order, at a gathering of believers, I received the answer to my question—"Right in front of you." I began in my circle of influence by speaking kindly to and about others. Then, I invited neighbors and friends, anyone interested, to meet for a weekly Bible study. This time, I did it the way I wish someone had done for me as a little girl, encouraging a personal relationship with Jesus above all else and a loving relationship among those people gathered in His name. Not everyone agreed or got along, but I was reminded to forgive others as Christ has forgiven me and keep showing up and reaching out—to keep imitating His grace. Understanding that a personal relationship with the Lord is what He wants with us, I now find myself waking up and praying, "Let me be your hands and feet. Show me the needs right in front of me. Give me the words to speak, and take me down the paths that serve you best." As a result, I've quit things that got in the way of my relationship with Him, things that weren't His best for me, and I began writing my own testimony for His glory—a daunting but rewarding task. I'm now a girl on a mission, working with Him instead of against Him.

The world constantly tries to convince us that this personal relationship with our Creator is not that important, but it's actually the most important and longest-everlasting relationship we'll have. Religion tells us that this relationship can only be fostered through other people, and that is simply a lie. God doesn't need man's intervention to speak with His children. When Moses led the Israelites out of captivity in Egypt to the Promised Land, God sent manna (daily bread) from the sky above to feed them. It was the reassurance of His continual provision for them (Deuteronomy 8:3). While we don't have manna falling from the skies, He still provides His daily bread—Jesus' words to store inside our hearts, recorded by the prophets and disciples as God's love letter to us. All we must do to nourish our souls is take the time to read them. We can also look up and around us to see evidence of Him. With this relationship, we can confess our sins to Him and seek His guidance. But to hear His voice, we first must listen. He wants us to get ready for the wedding. It's time to start inviting more guests!

God instructed Moses to demand the release of the Israelites from Pharaoh, just as Jesus commanded us to go get His people and demand their release from the devil. Redeemed and forgiven people, what on earth are we waiting for!? We know what it means to be free, and we have the keys. It's time to free our brothers and sisters, friends and enemies, neighbors and strangers, and let them out of captivity. It's time we take our faith and start

It's time we take our faith and start spreading it around like wildflower seeds.

spreading it around like wildflower seeds. It's time to be brave, like sons and daughters of the King of kings—equipped, prepared, and armored to the nth degree. When Jesus came, He searched for outsiders with a willing spirit, not impressive resumes. If you're willing, you're able. God whispers in our ears now, "Do you trust me with your heart?" If you can answer yes, lose your life, and you will gain a great reward. What kind of mercy and grace is this, you ask? It is the love of a heavenly Father, longing to return to His children so He can walk with them and talk with them.

When the Israelites wandered, God simply wanted them to acknowledge Him and obey. Are we also wandering and not acknowledging? Are we failing to hear His voice because we're not listening? What if He has been waiting on us rather than us waiting on Him? What if our desire to love Him above all things, trust Him with our hearts, acknowledge Him as the kinsman redeemer, and recognize Him as the lion and the lamb is really what He desires most? Maybe it's time we tear down all those church signs that divide us—holy whatever, second next to nothing, third this or that, first believer forever, the best and the last, etc.—and instead put up what unites us: Jesus Died For You. What if we start praying to have God show us His will for His people rather than for separate churches so that we can be more than our religions? God never created us for religion; He made us for relationships—His children. While in the name of goodness, we may serve Him, we may not be truly listening to Him or trusting in Him for what He wants from us or for us. Suppose we continue to exclude people from His love based on their failure to "fit in" (the steeples), affiliate (with a denomination), or assimilate (on the pews). We aren't universal or united in truth.

We don't have to change the Lord's ways—instead, learn to walk in them or maybe even walk on water with Him. By asking God to show us the way and the needs right in front of us, we may start loving Him above all else and our neighbors as ourselves, just as Jesus commanded. Then, we can't help but do His work and His will. We're bound to see a cloud of protection, a light in the darkness, and a lamp to our collective feet. We may find ourselves fighting for Him instead of against Him and, in an instant, walking with Him and talking face to face. Let's begin acting like His children whom He deeply loves, His sons and daughters, a royal court destined for heaven on Earth. "But you are a chosen people, a royal priesthood, a holy nation, God's special possession, that you may declare the praises of him who called you out of darkness into his wonderful light" (1 Peter 2:9).

Let's take down those signs that exclude and put up His name instead. Let's get off those pews, out from under those steeples, and lead the way out of captivity. If the name of Jesus offends, it is not because of what He did for us but what we didn't do with it. It's time to act like heirs to His holy throne—a bride worthy of Christ's return—and start genuinely, lovingly, and bravely inviting everyone to the wedding of a lifetime. Above all else, let us remember how great He is and that we don't need to build Him any more steeples. Let's go outside, into the world He created. We can trust He'll send us anywhere and everywhere He needs us to go, testifying to His greatness. If willing, He can show us the way through this modern wilderness. And while it's easy to love a beautiful church pew, it's not important to God. He never asked us to make up our own rules or stay seated.

"Then Jesus came to them and said, 'All authority in heaven and on earth has been given to me. Therefore go and make disciples of all nations, baptizing them in the name of the Father and of the Son and of the Holy Spirit, and teaching them to obey everything I have commanded you. And surely I am with you always, to the very end of the age.'"

~Matthew 28:18–20

REFLECTIONS:

1. What was your first experience with religion?
2. If you viewed yourself more as a child of God, how would it change your life?
3. What might keep you from trusting God?

Jenny Ingels is the mother of four "manimals," wife of a retired combat veteran, and a former federal agent. These varied life experiences exposed her to the lightest and darkest sides of the human condition, including the moment her best friend drank herself into a coma, which she never recovered from. It was then that she began reconsidering her own decades-long casual relationship with alcohol. It took ten more years and a breast cancer diagnosis before she finally threw away her drinking blanket. God's grace brought her to and through this life-altering transformation.

Recognizing what she learned could help save lives, she left her career to start the mission—*Pour It Out For Good.* Her podcast dives into the cultural influences, societal pressures, and biblical misconceptions that lead us to drink and keep us coming back for more and what we can do to change it for good.

"'For I know the plans I have for you,' says the Lord. 'They are plans for good and not for disaster, to give you a future and a hope. In those days when you pray, I will listen. If you look for me wholeheartedly, you will find me. I will be found by you,' says the Lord. 'I will end your captivity and restore your fortunes. I will gather you out of the nations where I sent you and will bring you home again to your own land.'"

~Jeremiah 29:11–14, NLT

CHAPTER 6

I Am More Than My Gift

By Jori O'Neale

What's your gift? If you had asked me this question ten years ago, my answer would have varied depending on my job or role in the church. I've done every type of job, from cashier to program manager, and over the last twenty-plus years as a Christian, I have served in every ministry in the church—all this without truly knowing my gift or calling. I know we are all called to share the good news (Matthew 11:28), but what was I *supposed* to be doing with my life? I meet women almost daily who walk around not knowing their gift, their calling, or their purpose. This question plagued me for decades, and my resume is proof of it. When we're young and in school, we are asked to make decisions about our careers and future occupations, but honestly, how can we? We have limited life experience, and as a Christian, I'm a firm believer that if we don't know God, the Creator of the universe, then we can't truly know ourselves, at least not well enough to fulfill our purpose and know our gift. Sisters, how many of you knew you could be saved and not sanctified—called by God but not content in Christ?

Before I lose you, stay with me for a moment. I am not suggesting a works-based faith, for it is by grace that we are saved, not by our works so that no man or *woman* can boast (Ephesians 2:8–9). What I am suggesting is that we take a good, hard look at the roles we play compared to the purpose we are to live out. For years, I found my identity in the titles

I carried—even in the church! Come on now; I know I'm not the only one. Serving in various ministries in leadership roles fed my ego to a great degree. I looked down on some and overlooked many, all in the name of effective leadership. Over the last three years, the Lord convicted me and caused me to examine my walk with Him more deeply. I had come to a dark place in my faith where I was going through the motions and just showing up.

Has that ever happened to you? I had a form of godliness but was denying the power of Christ in me. I want to share with you about my

Your walk with God is not about you!

gift—not how I discovered it but how God revealed it when I finally stopped trying to find it. Are you intrigued? Good! I have some hard truths to share, and I need you to be open to hearing them. Here is the first of them. Your walk with God is not about you! Likewise, my walk with God is not about me. This sounds odd to say, but it's not. And it's not about the rules, observances, or deeds done in the Christian faith. No, my friends, our walk with God is about much more than religion. It's about living out our purpose for those around us so they might reach out for Him and perhaps find Him. After trying my hand at every type of job out there, all legal, of course, God revealed that my gift was to teach and encourage. When I look back at every form of employment that I held, these two giftings stand out like sore thumbs. But how do I use these to preach and spread the gospel? As a high school teacher, this couldn't have been more evident in my classroom.

> *"'For I know the plans I have for you,' says the Lord. 'They are plans for good and not for disaster, to give you a future and a hope.'"*
> **~Jeremiah 29:11, NLT**

There was a knock at the door. "Jai, will you open the door for Jay R, please?"

I can say one thing about this kid: he was consistently inconsistent. His lack of attendance and refusal to complete assignments and participate were the reasons he was repeating my class. This time, he was coming more frequently, but he had missed so much work. I was honestly surprised he came to my class at all.

As he entered the room, I shouted out my usual greeting to him. "Hey, Jay R, welcome to class! Please sit with a group and grab a Chrome book. We're working on our presentations today."

He grabbed his laptop, sat in the front, and logged in. No headphones this time. He even asked the students next to him to share what we were doing and then proceeded to create a PowerPoint. Although surprised, I kept my composure and continued with the lesson.

Before the students left, I asked if anyone had any last words; this was a joke I made in all my health classes. But on this day, in particular, Jay R raised his hand.

"Yes, Jay R, how can I help you?" I asked.

"Are you a Christian?" he asked with a look of curiosity.

"Do you have any questions about the assignment, Jay R?" I redirected.

"You asked if we had any last words; I need to know if you're a Christian." His look told me I wasn't going to sidestep this question.

"I'm not sure what this has to do with the assignment, but yes, I'm a Christian." The entire class was now just as curious as I was about Jay R's line of questioning.

You're a real Christian, aren't you?

"You're a real Christian, aren't you?" This question made me smile. It was the same question I had asked my mentor at the Boys & Girls Club when I was sixteen.

I knew he was curious, and sensing that this might be the only opportunity to share my faith with the entire class without getting written up, I answered. "Yes, Jay R, I am a Christian. I believe that Jesus died on the cross, was buried, and rose again on the third day, and it's by faith through Him that we have eternal life."

"I knew it!" he exclaimed excitedly. "Can you pray for me?" Although this question gave me pause, I answered yes and asked if we could speak further in private.

I pulled a chair to his desk and asked what he needed to pray about. He told me that he had a court date set for the following Tuesday and that they were charging him with armed robbery, breaking and entering, and aggravated assault. Needless to say, I was speechless. He was only sixteen. I asked him what happened, and he began to tell me his story. He shared how he let a friend borrow his sneakers, but when he asked for them to be returned, his friend refused. Jay R said that he felt used and, as a result, enlisted the help of a few others to go rough his friend up a bit.

Jay R and I spoke for a while about better choices he could have made to avoid this incident. But the more I spoke with him, the more he no longer seemed like a kid who didn't enjoy school. Instead, he became a kid who was dealing with life, and school was just another added burden. Like so many other students, Jay R was looking to belong, the basic human desire we all share. He didn't feel like he belonged in his family or with his so-called friends. But in my class, the class he had to repeat, he came and participated and did the work.

I had become a safe space for Jay R, a place where he could be himself and experience love without condition. Whether he did my work or not, I still treated him with respect and always welcomed him to my class. I didn't do this so my principal would think highly of me or be the cool teacher; I did this because I believe that the love of Christ can penetrate any heart. I did this because my relationship with God is more than the religion I profess, the church I attend, or the ministry team I serve on. It's about more than showing up on Sundays or the size of the checks I write for tithes. My relationship with God is about sharing my God-given gift with everyone I come in contact with and exemplifying the love of Christ in every space I occupy. But it wasn't always like this. Allow me to share a bit of my life with you.

"In those days when you pray, I will listen."
~Jeremiah 29:12, NLT

As a young girl, I was raised in the church. My grandmother was a deaconess at the local Baptist church on the South Side of Chicago, Illinois. That meant I went to church each Sunday at 9:00 a.m. for Sunday school and didn't leave until 3:30 p.m. after the second service. Despite being in church all day Sunday, my life Monday through Saturday was anything but righteous. As I got older, the cruel reality of life began to rear its ugly head and caused me, at one point, to even question God's existence. I was in search of something . . . not a church home or a religion but purpose. I went from my grandmother's Baptist church to a Pentecostal church and later to a nondenominational church. I even frequented a Lutheran church for a bit. In each church, though some practices and sacraments differed, the overall feeling I got was the same. I would watch these people pray, praise, sing, share, and give on Sunday and then see them gamble, smoke, curse, and drink during the week. I didn't see anyone actually living out their beliefs, that is, until I met Niecey. And that is when my perspective changed.

Niecey was my aunt's long-time hair client and, most recently, my uncle's new girlfriend. She worked as the Boys & Girls Club director on the West Side of Chicago. During tenth grade, my aunt encouraged me to attend the Boys & Girls Club, where Neicey worked, and begin planning for college. One day, while accompanying Niecey to the local bodega, a man, hunched over and smelling of pure alcohol, stumbled into the store and came walking directly toward me. In an instant, Niecey stepped in front of me, and with the authority of Christ in her voice, she told the man, "I rebuke you in the name of Jesus. In the name of Jesus Christ, I command you to return to where you've come from, Satan. You have no authority here!"

She outstretched her hands and touched the man on his head, and he fell backward. He stumbled into the rack of potato chips, and when he got up, he looked confused. As he left the store, I turned to ask Niecey what had happened, but she continued with her purchase as though nothing had occurred. I didn't understand what I had just seen, but I learned later that I had witnessed someone get delivered. It wasn't on an altar or in the pews of my grandmother's Baptist church. It wasn't even on a Sunday. . . .

As we drove to the salon that night, I asked Neicey if she was a Christian. She asked me what I thought. I shared with her about the hypocrisy I saw in the church and how, though I believed in God, I was having a hard time trusting His people. She told me to pray about it and to ask God to make himself known to me.

Niecey walked with Jesus and, even more so, was living out her purpose, and that was evident in everything she did. She helped students in low-income neighborhoods find a safe place to be on Friday nights. Her work involved getting inner-city students jobs at nonprofits and local businesses. During the few years I had known her, Niecey had helped numerous students from the local neighborhoods not only obtain full rides to college but win multiple scholarships that provided them with a work-free college experience. That is what she ended up doing for me.

Niecey didn't go around preaching at people or telling them what they should and shouldn't do. Instead, she listened to them and offered her advice. She also made them feel comfortable enough to share absolutely anything with her. But, more than that, she showed me what it really meant to walk with Jesus and how powerful it could be when you walked in your gift and didn't reduce it to just being about a religion.

"If you look for me wholeheartedly, you will find me."
~Jeremiah 29:13, NLT

My quest for God was on. I began reading the Bible and putting what I read into practice. When I tested the Lord, He would always prove himself and show up for me in small and big ways. My life began to change. Seeing the impact that the Word of God had, I decided to switch my major from law to theology. On a random Monday, I saw an acceptance letter to Saint John's while going through my mail. I had never really thought about attending a Catholic university because it wasn't something I was familiar with. And though I had tried a lot of different churches and religious practices, none had included Catholicism. I opened the letter and saw that not only was there an acceptance letter inside but a financial breakdown that gave me more than 95 percent of my tuition. With the other scholarships that Niecey helped me secure, this was basically a free ride to college for the next four years. Considering this a sign from God, I signed the letter of acceptance and began making my plans to attend St John's University as a theology major.

During my first two weeks at St John's, the world sat still as the Twin Towers were attacked on 9/11. On that day, I witnessed Catholic and Protestant, Buddhist and Hindu, and Jewish Orthodox and Muslim students all join together in prayer for the lives lost. When tragedy struck, religion took a backseat, and love was all that remained. I spent the rest of that first semester studying world religions in and out of class, trying to determine what commonalities existed among them. Each time I read about a religion's origin, somehow, it always mirrored the story of Jesus Christ, the Son of God. This discovery caused me to read my Bible even more vigorously to learn about Jesus and how anyone could possibly be like Him.

> *"'I will be found by you,' says the Lord. 'I will end your captivity and restore your fortunes. I will gather you out of the nations where I sent you and will bring you home again to your own land.'"*
> **~Jeremiah 29:14, NLT**

One day after history class, a young man invited me to a Bible discussion on campus. Thinking it odd that this young man, who didn't seem to look very religious, was inviting me sparked my curiosity. When I arrived at the Bible discussion, my heart leaped. The entire room was filled with young people, Bibles in hand, talking about their walks with God and their understanding of the Word of God. I had seen this before—not in the physical but during my time in the Word of God. I was seeing Acts

2:42 lived out by young people. All of my prayers and my years of searching had led me to this point. Three weeks later, I gave my life to Christ.
I received the forgiveness of sins and

I buried my old life in the waters of baptism and arose a new creation.

the gift of the Holy Spirit. I buried
my old life in the waters of baptism
and arose a new creation. The Bible
tells us that anyone who belongs to
Christ has become a new person. "The old life is gone; a new life has
begun!" (2 Corinthians 5:17, NLT).

It was during my time at this Catholic university that God made himself known to me, showed me who He was, and, more importantly, revealed
to me who I was able to be in Him. This discovery did not come through
religious studies or any particular denomination. Instead, it occurred
when I turned away from the familiar and embraced the unknown. Here
are some things I did that may help you as well:

- Start journaling: Begin with a timeline of your life. On the timeline, insert any significant life events and memorable experiences.
  Spend time going through each of these events and write down
  the ways in which God was present. Continue this practice daily,
  if not weekly, to grow your faith and see God at work in your life.

- Pray without ceasing: I have found Psalm 143 especially helpful in
  times of doubt and confusion.

- Get a good Bible: I have found both the New International Version and the New Living Translation much simpler to understand.

- Find a community of like-minded individuals: The church I joined
  during my time at St. John's is the same one I attend to this day.

- Get some accountability: "All Scripture is God-breathed and is
  useful for teaching, rebuking, correcting and training in righ-
  teousness, so that the servant of God may be thoroughly equipped
  for every good work" (2 Timothy 3:16–17).

Today, I fully walk in my gift, and it is evidenced in my teaching and
preaching locally at women's events and through my functioning as an

ordained minister within my church. I host a weekly women's empowerment podcast for Christian women called *Thirty Minutes of Power* and work full-time as a high school teacher in the inner city schools of New York. One thing my students will tell you about Miss O'Neale is that she has a gift for making them feel seen and known. This gift comes from my time with the Lord, the One who sees me and knows me completely. I am not a religious woman; my relationship with God is more than a religion. It's more than my titles and even more than my gift. It's my life source and the thing that guides and energizes my choices, decisions, and actions.

REFLECTIONS:

1. In what ways have you put God in a box because of religion?
2. Who are the Jay Rs in your life that God sent to you so that they might learn about Him?
3. How can you make your walk with God more about the love of Christ and less about duty?

Jori O'Neale is an author, ordained minister, Bible teacher, and the CEO of IYH Innertainment LLC, a faith-based entertainment company created to spread the gospel through video and media. She is the wife to one amazing husband, mother to four miraculous children, and teacher to hundreds of NYC youth. Check out her podcast entitled *Thirty Minutes of Power*, which is dedicated to inspiring godly people to use their power to empower others.

"The gatekeeper opens the gate for him, and the sheep listen to his voice. He calls his own sheep by name and leads them out. When he has brought out all his own, he goes on ahead of them, and his sheep follow him because they know his voice . . . I know my sheep and my sheep know me."

~John 10:3–4, 14

CHAPTER 7

Knowing the Shepherd's Voice

By Rachel Rector

During my childhood, religion played a significant role in my life. I grew up in a Lutheran church, where the first step was being baptized as a baby. The second big step was attending three years of confirmation classes. I did not like these classes, as the videos were outdated, and I hated to get anything wrong (from answering questions to memorizing Bible verses). Although I didn't recognize it, I was already a people pleaser and caught up in the battle to live a "perfect" life. The final year of confirmation classes was very rigorous. Unlike the previous years, it was pastor-led. His teachings from *Luther's Small Catechism* were very dry, centered on the fear of going to hell, and highly saturated in memorizing Scripture without flaws. Once a week, we would stand up in front of our peers and individually recite the verse we had been given. If we didn't quote the verse perfectly, we would be shamed in front of the class and reminded that we had to pass with 100 percent accuracy before the confirmation date to be confirmed in the church. Thus, I focused on passing instead of truly hiding the Scriptures in my heart and storing them in my mind for future use.

When the day of my confirmation arrived, I thankfully passed and could partake in Communion. But instead of focusing on the true meaning of the Scriptures, it was just another check on the checklist of religion—baptism, check; confirmation, check; and now Communion, check. From a religious standpoint, I checked off all the boxes and looked like the model Christian. However, I didn't realize I had a God-sized hole just waiting to be filled by something other than another check.

Identity Wrecked

Fast forward one year. I was a freshman in high school. Usually, I rode the bus home, but that day, there was a last-minute opening for me to drive for my driver's education class. At the end of my driving session, my mom picked me up with a bewildered look. She explained that something horrible had happened at home, and she was so grateful that I had not been there. Little did I know that my driving session would end up saving my life or at least keeping me out of harm's way.

We pulled into the driveway, and I was unprepared for the devastation I was about to walk into. Burglars had invaded our home and traumatized our beloved dog. They had found a giant cement brick under our back deck—the deck I had sat on the day before, reading a book and soaking in the breathtaking country view—and had hurled the brick at our sliding glass door, causing it to ripple and shatter all over our kitchen floor.

My mom tried to prepare me for what I would see next and assured me we could leave at any time. I slowly made my way up the front steps and through the front door. Glass shards were strewn everywhere, and my poor dog was still trembling in fear. I walked up the stairs to a living room full of fingerprints, muddy footprints, and our personal belongings ripped to shreds.

Next came the walk down the hallway to my bedroom. This used to be a walk down memory lane, full of pictures from my parent's wedding, the births of my sister and me, and the smiling faces of beautiful family moments throughout the years. In an instant, these were replaced with an image forever imprinted in my mind. All of our treasured photographs had been torn to pieces. Picture frames had been shattered into more pieces than stars in the sky, and my heart was shattered as well.

The last stop was my bedroom. As I inched toward my bedroom door, I shook head to toe, dreading what I would see next. This was the place that I got to call mine. This was where my identity was created, and my most precious possessions were housed. My daybed was destroyed. The robbers had taken every last inch of my bed apart. My Precious Moments figurines and Beanie Babies displayed so neatly on my desk were gone. The Precious Moments girl that my great-grandma had kept in her display (representing me) was gone as well. As I scanned every nook and cranny of my room, distress, fear, and anger raged inside of me. The robbers even went as far as to take a basket full of my dirty laundry. To say I felt violated is a major understatement.

By now, my family was weeping over the utter devastation of our home. My mom quickly guided us out of the house and down the road to our neighbor's home. Our neighbors greeted us at the door and enveloped us with hugs. They then showed us to our beds, as we were exhausted. As my head hit the pillow, pictures of the vandalism in our home played like a motion picture. But a still, small voice soon broke through the noise and paused the movie. "Rachel, you have been living for all of your things. Those possessions do not define you. You are more than your things. You have been giving your whole life to your things. They were there yesterday and gone today. Stop living for material things. I am here! Live for me! 'Don't store up treasures here on earth, where moths eat them and rust destroys them, and *where thieves break in and steal.* Store your treasures in heaven, where moths and rust cannot destroy, and *thieves do not break in and steal*' (Matthew 6:19–20, NLT, emphasis added). I want a home in **you**."

Unlike my family, who woke up with fear in their eyes the following day, I awoke with determination in my eyes, determination to learn what it meant to live for the Lord instead of material possessions. Not long after, several girls at my school invited me to the next meeting of the Fellowship of Christian Athletes organization. At this meeting, I learned about an upcoming weekend retreat, and my parents agreed to let me go. This retreat was where I willingly gave my life to the Lord!

When My World Fell Apart

In the summer leading into my senior year of high school, my world fell apart. My parents separated, and my family no longer looked like the perfect nuclear family. On a daily basis, I found myself having to make hard decisions about my life, present, and future. Volleyball and tennis, which had brought me so much enjoyment, were cashed in for hours at work in hopes that I could save a little and still be able to attend college. My identity was being rocked again. . . . During this challenging time, I vividly remember putting my headphones on and walking down the lane from our house toward the gravel road while good and evil clashed in my mind, two voices battling for my attention. One was saying, "You don't have to stay here. You can end it all right now. Just take your life. No one is going to notice. You were not meant to go through all this pain." While the other countered with, "'For I know the plans I have for you,' declares the Lord, 'plans to prosper you and not to harm you, plans to give you hope and a future'" (Jeremiah 29:11).

At that moment, I had to make a decision. Was I going to listen to Satan, act on that thought, and end it all? Or would I trust the Lord and walk in the Scripture the Holy Spirit had spoken over me? In that instant, I chose. I blared Christian music on my portable CD player. Songs like "I Can Only Imagine," and other favorites filled the air as I shouted, "Away from me, Satan!" and walked in truth down the gravel road. As tears poured down my face, I sang at the top of my lungs and worshiped the Lord, trusting in His ways, His living and breathing Word, His provision, and the future He had for me.

Religion or Relationship

Time kept ticking, and I checked off more items on the religious checklist—get married, check, have one baby, check, multiply the earth, check, check, check. But after delivering four babies, giving up my dream job to stay at home with my children, and forgetting my first love (Jesus), I was burnt out and searching for identity again. I found myself knee-deep in checking off the boxes instead of living in a relationship with the one true God. While that part of my story can be found on my website, www. beautifuljoyrachel.com, for the remainder of this chapter, I want to dive deep into what God has shown me over the past two years.

On January 2, 2023, I woke up to God telling me to leave our Lutheran church and take our family to a Bible-based church close to our home. I responded that I would listen to His instructions but needed my husband to agree. I jumped out of bed and shared the idea with my husband hesitantly. I was genuinely expecting him to say no. He had grown up attending the Lutheran Church and school and was surrounded by an extended family of devout Lutherans. Surprisingly, he agreed to go the following day.

The first Sunday we attended, an elementary-aged child was baptized. My deep-thinking daughter approached me at home after the service and said, "Mom, how come some churches baptize babies while others baptize all ages?" I thanked her for asking, and we discussed the baptism beliefs taught in Christian religions. Then she turned and asked, "What does the Bible say about baptism?" Together, we opened the Bible and began to read.

"Mom, it doesn't say anything about baptizing babies," she reflected.

"You are right, sweet girl, it doesn't command us anywhere to baptize babies. That is a belief of some religions," I affirmed.

The following week, my sweet girl happily shared everything she had learned in Sunday school. And then she gazed up into the air, which usually means she is contemplating something, and said, "Mom, today in Sunday school, they offered Communion to all of us. I told them I didn't want to take it because I hadn't learned about it and needed your permission." So we opened the Bible to 1 Corinthians 11:24–29 and discussed the Lord's Supper. After our conversation, I contacted a few pastors of Bible-based (as opposed to religion-based) churches. I sought their wise counsel on Communion, how to teach our children about Communion, and if the Bible teaches an appropriate time for children to start taking Communion. As discussed earlier, I had undergone rigorous confirmation training as a child, but it was not fully biblically based. Instead, it was heavily based on Lutheran precepts. These conversations led me to seek out kingdom-centered speakers, pastors, and authors who made me dive deeper into the Word and question everything I had been taught.

> **This journey of discovery ultimately turned most of what I believed on its head.**

This journey of discovery ultimately turned most of what I believed on its head.

One morning, I performed my regular routine. I had read my Bible, check, my devotional, check, and prayed, check. At the end of my prayer, I heard a still, small voice say, "Are you done yet? Are you ready to listen now?"

"What, Lord?" I questioned, "I prayed for my whole family as well as friends that I promised I would pray over."

"Oh, sweet Rachel," the Lord said. "All of those are heard, but you are missing the most important thing—listening to my voice. Have you even asked me what I wanted for your day?"

This was a major gut punch. I had been so focused on checking off all the boxes and doing the "right" thing that I didn't leave room for the most important thing—allowing God to share His plans for me and the Holy Spirit to guide me.

Listening for His Voice

This early-morning conversation led me on an adventure. For months, I leaned in, longing to hear His voice instead of simply following a routine and checking off all the boxes on what a "good" Christian should do. The book of John addresses this powerfully.

> *"The gatekeeper opens the gate for him, and the sheep listen to his voice . . . When he has brought out all his own, he goes on ahead of them, and his sheep follow him because they know his voice."*
> **~John 10:3–4**

"I know my sheep and my sheep know me."
~John 10:14

Living for the Lord is **more than a religion.** It is more than a list of good works that we need to check off every day. Imagine for a moment that your daughter wanted to talk to you. As you patiently waited, she took a shower and dressed herself in a stunning outfit. She brushed and fixed her hair until it was model-perfect. She ate a nutritious breakfast and brushed her teeth. She sat down to read a book on being the best child. And after she had completed all the "proper" steps, she put on her high heels and ran to you to demand everything she needed. She then went on her merry way, never stopping for a moment to ask you for advice or listen to the direction and wisdom you wanted to give her. Did she even listen to your voice? No! Did you expect her to do all the above before coming to you? No!

God doesn't want something from you. He wants something for you.

Priscilla Shirer explains in her book *Fervent* that Satan wants you to believe that your value is based on all the things you do. He wants all these "things" to fill up our schedules and replace our much-needed time with God. She states that "God doesn't want something from you. He wants something for you." And she reminds us that just because something is "good" does not mean it is from God and that "even good things can culminate into slavery." By crowding our schedule with all the "good" things, we do not leave space for His voice.

So, just like us, God does not expect His children to have it all together before coming to Him. Instead, He longs for us to slow down, lean into Him, listen for His voice, and follow His lead.

Complete Surrender

Crystal Paine taught me in *The Time Saving Mom* that I need to *surrender* my day to Him and ask for His help every day. On the days I do this, things run a lot smoother, and my mind is set on His will instead of checking off all the boxes. Kingdom entrepreneur Gail Root shared with me in her Master Your Morning Challenge that we should start our morning routine by listening to His voice. When I first began implementing this challenge, one of two things happened: I fell asleep in my chair, or my mind wandered to my to-do list. Now, after more practice, I find that it steers my mind to the parts of my day that I need to pray over, facilitates quiet downloads from Him about my day, or brings my attention to other things He wants me to do—such as this chapter.

In Pedro Adao's 2023 Wisdom Challenge, speaker and pastor Michael Dalton exclaimed, "What we are taught by religion is a way to *exist,* but what we were taught by Jesus is the way to *overcome.*" Do you just want to exist, or do you want to overcome? God doesn't want us to just exist by following all the "correct" religious practices; instead, He wants to produce greatness in you and overcome the world.

In Revelation 3:20, Jesus shouts, "Here I am! I stand at the door and knock. If anyone hears my voice and opens the door, I will come in and eat with that person, and they with me." God invites you to sit at His table and take in His nourishing food, provision, and blessings. He wants two-way conversation and an intimate relationship with you. My friend, put down your to-do list. But hear me out; although reading the Word and praying are avenues for hearing God's voice, you need to take inventory of your heart posture. Are you doing something (reading your Bible, praying, journaling, etc.) to check off a box, or are you doing it to draw nearer to Jesus and hear His voice?

What a joy life will be if we choose to slow down, talk less, listen more, and open our eyes to the gifts and blessings the Lord is waiting to share with us. Sweet one, stop striving and existing just to complete all the religious "right" steps and instead start resting at His table, leaning into His arms, and listening to His voice. "When a woman hears God's voice and obeys Him, she's powerful," Priscilla Shirer declares in her book *He Speaks to Me.* Put on your armor, listen to Him, and take your place of power in this battle called life not as the perfect _____ (insert religion) but as the royal daughter of the one true King!

REFLECTIONS:

1. Where do you find your identity? Are you looking within or searching for your identity in external things?
2. Are you doing _____ (reading your Bible, praying, etc.) to check off a box, or are you doing it to draw near to Jesus and hear His voice?
3. Are you surrendering your heart and will, listening for His voice, and acting on what He has shared? Or are you taking steps based on your fleshly will?

Rachel Rector is a compassionate encourager and trailblazer. She holds true to her childhood nickname, firecracker. Once God lights a fire in her heart, she is unafraid to step out and walk in God's calling for her and her family. She has blazed the path as a kindergarten teacher, a K-5 ELL teacher, a network marketing team leader for two companies, and an accountability coach and partnership coordinator for a top marketing and virtual event company.

She is mainly known for her God-given gift of mercy, helping all who meet her feel seen, heard, and valued. A common phrase she hears is, "I do not know why I shared all that with you. I have never shared that before." She is on a mission in her home, blog, books, and anywhere God leads her next to help women and girls reclaim hope, identity, and joy.

More THAN My Past

"Yet who knows whether you have come to the kingdom for such a time as this?"

~Esther 4:14, NKJV

CHAPTER 8

Her Tears Unlocked Her Story

By Teresa Holbrooks Nichols

"The deadline's when? Next week, you say? Surely that can't be true!" You see, this person who signed up to write a chapter about being more than her past somehow disappeared at the most inopportune time. Anxiously, she wondered how she could be that confident in the beginning and yet feel so unsure of herself and her abilities now.

Even so, she could still see that woman who boldly stepped in front of the camera to say, "Hi, my name is Teresa, and I am more than a wife, more than a mother, more than my job titles, and I am definitely more than my past!" Honestly, it had felt really good to get that off her chest in that unplanned moment!

Admittedly, the encouragement of the women surrounding her while speaking their truths had helped her step out of her comfort zone, and she had amazed herself by doing such a thing. "Where are those sweet ladies when I need them?" she asked herself as she tangibly sensed her self-doubt building within. She could certainly use a little nudge from those enthusiastic women right about now!

She had sought wisdom and direction, knowing that her help came from the Lord, yet was disappointed because she was not hearing His voice in this time of desperation. All semblance of confidence was dwindling steadily, and she knew this was most assuredly not the time for it! It was almost laughable as she recalled how many times she'd picked up a pen, put it to paper, and tried to write her story. Every attempt she had made seemed right at first but afterward left her feeling dissatisfied.

Her normal frustrations seeped in, and, as usual, her confusion increased. This behavior was predictable for her, to say the least. She felt herself sinking into the abyss of indecisiveness that plagued her life so often. Teetering between the positives and the negatives was her norm. Feelings of being unworthy, unqualified, and inadequate quickly rushed to the forefront of her mind. It's almost like it was integrated into her DNA at this point.

She began to hear the little whispers that were so familiar, telling her that she should just give up, and frankly, she was tempted to do just that. What was she possibly thinking? How in the world could she write

She recognized that the hardships she had endured only made her stronger and wiser.

about being more than her past and convince someone else to believe it when she still struggled to accept it for herself? For weeks, she had tried and failed to portray a picture of a successful and confident woman who had overcome her past and gotten through the trials she had faced. It was like being on a teeter-totter of emotions. . . . On one side, she could easily see victorious breakthroughs to celebrate; yet, on the other side, she still faced areas that remained unresolved and quite challenging. This mixture of truths made it difficult to write her story.

She recognized that the hardships she had endured only made her stronger and wiser. Yet—she admitted—she would not have chosen them for herself. The dilemma now stemmed from the problems that were not yet resolved, which thwarted her attempts to write about being "more than enough."

Without a doubt, thoughts of past traumatic events were not easy to face. In each episode that came to mind, time seemed to stand still and drag out the consequences, disrupting the everyday cadence of life as she knew it. In those exact times, however, she could clearly testify of God's faithfulness and His uncanny ability to show up for her at precisely the right moment—more times than she could count.

"So where is God now?" she quipped, immediately feeling guilty for such thoughts as she let her mind drift to the familiar path where she wondered if God was mad at her. Her emotions quickly began to run rampant, bombarding her with negativity and thoughts of how she had disappointed God. This was a well-worn and slippery slope, and once descending along this path, it was extremely difficult for her to escape. Admittedly, this had always been the exact kind of moment when she would begin to believe that she was not enough, and it was happening again—in total opposition to the intended purpose with which this all began.

Had she misunderstood God? Was He not yet ready for her to step into the role of author? Confusion now reigned supreme and had her in the bewildering predicament of not knowing what to do next. But, one thing she did know, the excitement and determination of writing her story had faded.

It's not like she had not been patiently waiting for the words to flow. She had made dozens of attempts over the last few months to declare what had been clear to her on day one when she stepped in front of that camera. Procrastination was not the culprit either. She had spent hours trying to accomplish the task at hand. Sleepless nights and stacks of edited pages were proof of her diligence in trying to fulfill the assignment.

But nothing she had written so far even implied that she was more than enough. On the contrary, the central repeating topic seemed to be insinuating the opposite, no matter how many times she started over. The insecurities she carried were unyielding and strenuous, just as the enemy intended them to be. Years of warfare in this area had still not effectuated complete resolution, and every attempt to write something different brought on a barrage of bad memories and accusations of past failures.

Days away from the deadline and doubting her ability to accomplish what she had set out to do, she had to admit that she was not gaining ground. In fact, she felt stuck and headed for failure. It wasn't supposed to be like this, of that she was sure! That eager, overjoyed woman, who couldn't wait for the chance to become a published author, was now feeling foolish and, in her frustration, relented to the tears she could no longer contain. The enormity of the battle demanded a reaction, and though it seemed odd, crying actually felt good. It was as if her anxious thoughts evaporated one by one with each tear that splashed upon her cheeks.

She was reminded of a Bible verse that said, "You keep track of all my sorrows. You have collected all my tears in your bottle. You have recorded each one in your book" (Psalm 56:8, NLT), and she sensed the love of God enveloping her in her moment of weakness. It was tremendously comforting to feel His presence while realizing that He knew her tears would be the key to releasing her innermost worries and fears.

In her heart, she knew she had been given an immensely valuable opportunity to step toward her biggest dream, but there she was, crying about it. What in the world had caused such an uncontrollable outpouring of sadness and desperation? Perhaps it was the tremendous weight of years of pent-up doubt and insecurity that now had her emotions overflowing and had her sniffling repeatedly, resembling a woman whose life was in shambles.

She couldn't help feeling guilty and even a little ashamed of the tears despite the fact that they had brought her His immediate comfort. God had done so much to propel her towards her long-held dreams of writing, and she knew she should be "rejoicing in victory," not "wallowing in defeat."

Suddenly, the thought hit her that the enemy must think he was winning the battle, which did not sit well with her! The seriousness of her plight was clearly evident, and though it would not be easy, she would lean into her faith for the strength needed to proceed. It had never disappointed her before, nor would it disappoint her now! And once again, a Bible verse came to mind: "God is within her, she will not fall" (Psalm 46:5), and a spark of hope ignited.

So the question remained. . . . Was she more than her past, or was she not? What was it that was holding her back? An immense sense of vulnerability filled her heart with trepidation, and she perceived something she knew was contributing to her problem: it simply felt wrong to proclaim that she was more than her past when many unresolved issues still plagued her life. She had spent years believing that, until she saw victories in very specific areas, she could not take steps toward her dreams.

The tactics employed by the enemy had hit their intended targets for way too long and had her bound. It was as though she had been waiting for a perfect life before she could begin to share her story—which was simply ridiculous but effective all the same! When she finally concluded that God could actually use her through the trials, it was like a weight lifted from her chest. She no longer had to wait until the battles had been won. Goodness gracious, that was a relief!

It was as though she had been waiting for a perfect life before she could begin to share her story.

Yet, almost simultaneously, regret washed over her as she thought about how much time she had wasted believing the lie. That time could have been spent more effectively if only she'd known the truth. Thankfully, God quickly assured her that there was purpose in every detail of her journey, and He would use it all for good.

But the enemy was not going to give up so easily. Another accusation hit her mind and had her wondering, "Am I too old to start new things?" Smiling and almost laughing, she realized that with her age came decades of material to work with! Aha! She sensed the quirky side of herself emerging from the shadows, and it was about time!

She paused to reflect and remembered repeatedly writing a specific phrase in her journals. Quickly, she rushed to pull one of them out to confirm and read the words, "You are uniquely constructed for such a time as this!" There's a story behind the "uniquely constructed" portion of that quote, but that was not the focus of the day—instead, the words *for such a time as this* captured her attention. In her heart, it felt like God was confirming that He had opened the doors of opportunity for her to write this story right now. All those times that she had written those words over the last several months or had them come to her mind were preparing her heart for what God had planned for her to accomplish. She had even been toying with the idea that "for such a time as this" would one day be part of a book title and again sensed confirmation of its importance for things to come. She thought of Queen Esther and how she was positioned perfectly to fulfill God's plan. God had a plan for Esther's life and revealed it in His timing.

Applying Esther's story back to her own had her now acknowledging that every moment of her life had been seen by God and known by God. Even the undesirable things she had lived through would have a purpose. God had His reasons, and they were far beyond her ability to understand. She was humbled and realized that this would be where the trusting part of faith was required.

Her bold choices to write about being more than her past were finally taking center stage in her mind once again. She knew the battle was not entirely over but sighed as a bit of confidence returned . . . just in the nick of time. She must do this. She must convince herself, her family, her friends, and those who would read this book that she is more than her past.

Suddenly, she sensed that a little shift had begun to take place in her thoughts. Although the enemy had fought against her efforts to put her words to paper, she now felt hope returning—moving her closer to that confident and excited woman who had embraced this wonderful opportunity months before.

At that moment, specific memories from decades before rushed into her mind, and although she did not understand their purpose, she would be forever grateful for what they would reveal. . . . She saw herself as she was then, a young girl struggling with thoughts that she was not good enough. Worry consumed her as far back as she could remember. And though it wasn't something that most people thought a child of that age would be going through, it was her story.

She remembers that when her parents divorced, her life shifted. It became a little more challenging to be the "happy-go-lucky" little girl she had been before. She vividly recalled feelings of guilt and hidden sadness that stemmed from her innermost concerns about each of her parents. When she was with her mom, was her dad mad, sad, or lonely? Her concern for him was intensified by the fact that he was deaf, and her ability to communicate with him was limited. As a result, she had no way of knowing how he felt.

On the other hand, if she had fun while with her dad, she was concerned that her mom might be upset with her somehow. Her mom never gave her reasons to feel this way, nor did she ever dissuade her from going to see her dad, so she couldn't explain where the feelings stemmed from. She simply felt like something wasn't right and desperately wanted them to love her and know how much she loved them.

Honestly, her mind never stopped wondering how she was making them feel, even into adulthood. She realized now that they probably weren't concerned about the things she imagined. But it never changed that she always felt like she was disappointing one of them. This left her feeling very insecure at a young age. And those feelings contributed to her desire to prove her love and prove she was worthy of being loved. It was instinctual, never spoken, yet never truly resolved. She felt the need to earn love and acceptance, whether it was required of her or not. It just was what it was!

Those types of scenarios continued throughout her lifetime. The need to be more, achieve more, and accomplish more drove her. She may not have recognized it early on, but it was all part of the effort to prove she was enough because she felt the exact opposite most of the time. This concept of "proving herself" was something she had spent most of her life trying to accomplish in one way or another. And it was not because anyone specifically asked it of her, mind you. Instead, it was a deeply rooted need to prove things to herself and others. It had been there for as long as she could remember. It was exhausting, but it was a huge part of who she was.

Her next thoughts had her fast-forwarding to a traumatizing and unexpected event that truly devastated her self-confidence. She had married at nineteen and was in the seventh year of marriage when her husband came home to tell her he was leaving. He had met another girl at work that he wanted to be with. To say that this new revelation floored her would definitely be an understatement. From her point of view, things were pretty good at the time. They were even trying to start a family, and her excitement was boundless. Little did she know that while she was full of hope that she would soon be pregnant, he was choosing to walk away.

His decision rocked her entire world and shattered everything she had believed to be true about the direction of her future. She recalled having prayed many times as a young girl that she would never have to go through a divorce. She had been adamant in those prayers and recalled them vividly, even now. And though her faith had taught her that divorce was not an option, there she was, facing that exact scenario—by no choice of her own. But although she was devastated by her partner's decision, the root of her pain went much deeper. She felt like her faith had been shaken to the core.

She questioned God about why He had allowed this to happen to her, but the answers did not come. To be honest, she was deeply hurt, and feelings of anger, confusion, and annoyance swirled within her. She was bewildered by the circumstances she was facing and the fact that God had not intervened on her behalf. She needed His help; where was He?

Through the pain and whirl of these emotions, however, one irrefutable fact remained. . . . She was not good enough for the man she'd married. His betrayal had touched the deepest parts of her soul, and the humiliation alone had been a horrible thing to endure. She wondered if she would ever be able to hold her head high again. The brokenness caused by those long-ago moments of betrayal, heartache, and uncertainty fueled her insecurities and had her constructing walls of protection around her heart that remain today . . . just in case someone ever decides she is not enough again.

After some time had passed, God revealed the fact that He had not ignored her prayers. There had been a second part to those prayers—the part where she had begged God never to let her own children experience the divorce of their parents like she had. She now saw that God had protected her from that possibility by the timing of all that transpired. He had not deserted her in the trial; honestly, her faith needed that confirmation.

Looking back over the years, she saw instances where she had been broken and hurt many times. This time, instead of just feeling the pain, she was seeing things through a different lens, one where God's faithfulness was evident all along. She sighed and whispered to herself, "I'll be forever grateful for God's deliverance in the toughest of times!" Expressing those words may have been the key to unlocking what she had been looking for all along. She breathed deeply and

I'll be forever grateful for God's deliverance in the toughest of times!

allowed the assurance and strength inspired by that statement to sink in. God himself had proven to her time and time again that He was worthy, faithful, and to be trusted!

This look into the past (with its ups and downs, triumphs and failures) helped her face the fact that she *had* changed through the years. Though many parts of her remained the same, many more had adapted and grown. She could now see that God had not wasted anything. Instead, He had used the events of her life to get her attention and teach her things she would need to know for the next chapter.

Her past had threatened to defeat her, and all the years of trying to prove herself worthy while also trying to please others had taken their toll. But she had not given in. And those behaviors, though difficult and exhausting at times, were tightly woven into the core of her identity, necessary and important parts of who she was and who she is now. It's what she knows—what makes her the resilient woman she is today.

She finally wanted to scream out the declaration that she was indeed more than her past! God had made her victorious thus far, and even though challenges remained, she felt confident—not in her ability but in His—He would redeem her past!

At last . . . her story felt right and ready to submit. But she couldn't help but wonder why her words flowed when she began writing about herself as though she were a different person. She had no explanation, but she trusted that God would reveal the reason in His Timing. Until then, she would keep reminding herself that God uses all things for His Glory, and this would forever be part of her story. He was not done with her yet. And she was extremely thankful that, once again, God's perfect timing allowed her to complete the mission of proving to herself, and hopefully to you, that she is more than her past—She is more than enough! Story to be continued . . .

REFLECTIONS:

Consider writing down your answers to these questions. Then, post them, pray over them, and ask God to reveal them in His timing!

1. How might the tactics of the enemy deceive you?
2. Do you believe you are here "For Such a Time as This?" What dreams are you holding close to your heart?
3. Do you feel unable to fulfill your calling and purpose?

Teresa Holbrooks Nichols juggles many different titles. She is a wife, mother, licensed residential builder, general contractor, real estate agent, and owner/partner of D&T Custom Homes. She excitedly adds *author* to that list by becoming an author contributor for *More Than Enough* alongside five-time best-selling author and publisher Tamra Andress. She is the creator of *Uniquely Constructed* and writes a column by that name for the Patheos Evangelical Channel, Facebook, and Instagram. She is a member of Compel Training at Proverbs 31 Ministries and has attended "A Day for Writers with Lysa TerKeurst" and "She Speaks" (an annual conference that helps women "find, own, and use their voices to make an eternal impact"). She knows God is propelling her toward her dreams of writing and publishing and trusts in His timing. Her ultimate goal is to become exactly who God uniquely created her to be! She cherishes faith and family and continuously reminds them by saying, "I love you more than words can say."

"Rejoice not over me, O my enemy, when I fall, I shall rise, when I sit in darkness, the Lord will be a light to me. I will bear the indignation of the Lord because I have sinned against him, until he pleads my cause and executes judgment for me. He will bring me out to the light, I shall look upon his vindication."

~Micah 7:8–9, ESV

CHAPTER 9

Shame Doesn't Win This

By Samantha Reimold

Honestly, when I started writing this, I didn't feel worthy. I am still going through a difficult season, but this is my reality and my struggle with sin, guilt, and shame. Almost as soon as I resolved to write down this part of my story, God decided to take me on a spiritual journey that I was not expecting. But through it, I have deeply understood God's mercy and goodness. And that is not the same thing as receiving no earthly consequences. Instead, it is being able to see Him no matter the consequences, a truth, I am sad to say, that took me a long time to understand.

I honestly have no idea how you will feel after reading my story or what you will think of me, but what God has taught me through the journey of writing this is that I love you all, and I do pray that what I write helps you in some way or can connect with you in some way. But even if you choose to judge me and my past at the end, it's okay. I forgive you because God has forgiven me, and it has taken me a really long time to believe that truly.

I have always tended to be more of a people pleaser/controller—wanting to help others and make sure that everyone was happy and cared for. I would always let others choose when there was a decision to be made, and confrontation was something I shied away from. Not that I didn't stand up for myself, but I just never cared to go against the grain. I was always happy doing what made others happy. Even to this day, my poor husband is the only one I regularly disagree with. Love you, babe. And it is still difficult for me to do something solely for myself.

While all of these are more personal issues than sins, they do intertwine with some lifelong struggles I've had with feelings of guilt: the guilt of doing anything for myself without feeling selfish, the guilt when I go once a year to get my hair done and it takes three hours that I could have spent caring for my family, the guilt when I'm tired and want to relax but the kids want to play, the guilt that I should give my husband more attention but some days I'm just mentally exhausted, the guilt that I don't see my friends or my parents or my brother and his family enough. Ahhhhhh, It's just too much. It's this constant struggle between trying to do everything for everyone and not being able to say no (because I might let them down) that is so exhausting—as are the continuous attempts to keep everyone happy, safe, and loved and the guilt I always feel when I inevitably fail. . . . I can't be everyone's happiness. I can't keep everything together all the time. And I can't continue to carry this incessant guilt; it is suffocating.

Over the years, I had gotten very used to the cycle of feeling great while taking care of everyone and being overcome with guilt when I didn't meet the expectations I'd set for myself. But it wasn't until more recently that I also began to experience the soul-crushing pain of another scary emotion—shame. But what is the difference between guilt and shame? I was listening to a podcast by pastor, missionary, and teacher Rachael Groll entitled *Hearing Jesus*, where she talked about the difference between the two. She explained that guilt is the feeling that we made a mistake, no matter how small or large, while shame is the feeling that we *are* the mistake. Ugh, my heart still aches when I think of the way shame has made me see myself at times.

A friend recently led me to a book by Brené Brown called *Atlas of the Heart*, where she says that "shame thrives in secrecy, silence, and judgment." As hard as it may be, this is me not hiding in the secrecy and silence anymore. There are whole seasons of my life that I lived in this state, a state of secrecy, a state where I hid any part of me that could be perceived as broken or faulty, a state of never speaking of my mistakes and just internalizing them, a state where I felt if anyone really knew me, they would be disgusted. I couldn't let people know the sins that I struggled with because then they would never see me in the same way. And I could not bear that judgment because the judgment I already placed on myself and others (thinking they were better than me) was already too heavy. How can they always seem to do the right thing? How can they always be so put together? How are they so much closer to God? I didn't realize all of these thoughts and emotions swirling inside me were connected. And I always felt like I needed to be better, do better, do more. The thought that I could actually control my own life and the things around me if I just tried harder, had more money or helped more people overwhelmed me. I put so much pressure on myself that I couldn't help but fall back into the guilt and shame pit eventually.

Shame separates us from God. It is so powerful, and it is the devil's way of making us tear ourselves down from the inside out. It makes us feel isolated and alone. It destroys our relationships with ourselves, with others, and most importantly, with God. It is a scary, isolating place, and it is dark. Unfortunately, too many of us get lost there. When we are in that darkness of feeling isolated and alone, when we think that there is no way that anyone could love us or even want to be around us because of things we've done or continue to do, when we cause pain and bring hardship to our family and the people we love—we just can't climb out on our own.

"O my God, in you I trust; let me not be put to shame; let not my enemies exult over me."
~Psalm 25:2, ESV

I have been a Christian all my life in the sense that I always knew that if you do good things, you go to heaven, and if you do bad things, you go to hell. I had heard that Jesus forgives and that He died on the cross for my sins, but honestly, I never really thought about the depth of love contained in that statement. I very much took Jesus for granted. And as I write that, I am pushing away those feelings of guilt for my past self not caring more. He forgives me, and I forgive myself.

I say this because I did and do know right from wrong. I have always known that to hurt others is a sin. So, looking back on this most recent season of my life, I still don't really understand how I allowed myself to be a person I am so ashamed of. Somewhere along the way, my vision of right and wrong got lost—or maybe not even that. . . . There were things I was doing that I knew were wrong, but I did them anyway. I found myself stealing—from people I loved and cared about. There is no explanation I will ever be able to think of, at least that I know of today, to explain why. The first time it happened, I felt such immediate guilt that I almost came clean right away, but time passed, and no one noticed. Somehow, I could flip a little switch in my brain and almost wholly forget it happened.

But, randomly, something would remind me, and I would have as close to a panic attack as I'd ever experienced. I would be sick to my stomach. I would close my eyes and try to get that switch to flip again so that I wouldn't remember. I would pray to God to please take my sin away, to help me not be this person, to help me not hurt the people I cared about. And eventually, the switch would flip, and the guilt would dull. But then it would happen again. I would take more—and then again. I just remember praying to God to please help me beat the devil in my head, to please give me the strength to stop. I prayed for the strength to rely on Him and not myself. And I prayed to please make it right, and He did. . . .I was caught. I was questioned, and I panicked, so I lied. How could I reveal this to my family, to anyone who knew me? So it continued . . . more sinning and even more guilt. But now that guilt was transforming into shame. I was this monster, this person that, if someone else had told me they had done these things, would have judged them. What kind of Christian was I?—one whose soul was going to hell, for sure.

Guilt is there to help you know you have done wrong, to help guide you back to God and to give you the courage to make things right. Shame, however, can play crazy, awful tricks on you and your perception of reality. There have been entire generations wiped out because of shame. In her podcast *Hearing Jesus*, Rachael Groll recalled a mission trip to East Africa, where she visited a church with many children but only the pastor and one grandmother to care for them. When she asked the grandmother where all of the parents were, she was told that most of them had died from HIV. That in itself didn't really shock me; I had heard about how rampant and deadly this disease can be. And so, in my mind, I pictured a remote town with limited resources or education about the disease. But that was not the case.

Rachael went on to share that the saddest part was the realization that UNICEF was there. There was aid and education readily available. There was a medication that could give these people long and happy lives. So why were they still dying? Shame. In their culture, being found to have HIV would bring shame on them and their entire family. So they were choosing to die. As Rachael says, "The reality of dying was better for them than the shame that would come on their family." My heart broke. How can this feeling, this fear of other's opinions, actions, and consequences take so much from God's children?

But it does, and it has in my own life. My personal feelings of shame and guilt took me to a place where I just didn't know who I was anymore. How could I look at my husband when I had tricked him? He thought he was married to this amazing person, but he had no idea who I really was. How could I mother my children when I was such a hypocrite, telling them to do the right things, to be kind, and not to hurt others. . . . I felt like an imposter in church and around my friends. No one could love this person I was, not truly. I even felt guilty for having moments of joy or happiness, as though experiencing any happy moment would diminish what I had done and the hurt I had caused. I was too ashamed to even pray to God. There were days I had to sit with my Bible in my lap and force myself to open it. I was so afraid to read the verses He might show me like Proverbs 2:21–22 (ESV): "For the upright will inhabit the land, and those with integrity will remain in it, but the wicked will be cut off from the land, and the treacherous will be rooted out of it." All I could hear was—Am I the wicked one the Bible speaks of? And how could I come back from that?

I prayed to see His heart, His grace, His love, and His character in everything.

How self-centered was I? I was looking for myself in every passage I read, praying for guidance, punishment, or forgiveness. What I was missing, though, was God's character in what I was reading, and I had to lean into Him more than ever. I prayed for God to help me understand the things I had done, understand who I truly was, and where my heart was. I prayed to see His heart, His grace, His love, and His character in everything. That is when I started to see a small light in the darkness. I needed more of Him. And thankfully, even while I was drowning in shame, God is merciful. He was at work for my soul as He is for yours.

"For by grace you have been saved through faith. And this is not your own doing; it is the gift of God."
~Ephesians 2:8, ESV

God wants us to have a community. He does not want us to be alone. And without me realizing it, He walked my family into a community that would help to save my life. He gave me people to share my pain with, people who would start to teach me what God's heart truly is, and I began to understand that there was nothing I could do to earn His love. No matter how many people I helped or how much I gave of myself to others, there was no point system. (Yes, He wants you to grow in His likeness, but I was not doing these things to earn His love. That had already been given.) We are all saved by grace through our faith in Him. Even the worst of us. This community consisted of people who stepped up to help me, people who were broken in their own way and in true need of Him. But they freely shared their stories and their brokenness, which helped to show me how important having a community in Christ can be. In the middle of some of the worst shame I have ever felt in my life, God surrounded me with these people. When I prayed for relief, God gave me courage, the courage to reach out to friends to pray for me, the courage to reach out for help. And each responded with encouragement and godly wisdom. They led me to articles and scriptures to learn what true repentance meant and how I did not have to live in this shame forever. And I know they prayed for me because I felt it. I felt the weight beginning to lift. Their kindness and love will never be forgotten.

> *"Again, when a wicked person turns away from the wickedness he has committed and does what is just and right, he shall save his life. Because he considered and turned away from all the transgressions that he had committed, he shall surely live; he shall not die."*
> **~Ezekiel 18:27–28, ESV**

I had to make some really difficult decisions. I had to accept the reality that the pain on this earth could never be greater than eternal separation from God. And then I had to be honest with the ones I had hurt. I had to confess to them and to God. I had to stop this sin and commit my heart to change. I had to ask God for forgiveness and accept that God's forgiveness of my sins did not mean that I would not have earthly consequences. I had to understand that the consequences I received for my actions had nothing to do with God's goodness and the goodness He still wanted for me. And I had to hold on to His truth that no matter the earthly consequence, my eternity with Him had already been secured. I could be forgiven. You can be forgiven—truly forgiven. Accepting peace from God

Sometimes, it is the struggle itself that truly is the blessing. For that is what can bring us back.

does not diminish the things you have done or the people you have hurt, but God still wants good for you. You can use your pain, your suffering, and your blessings to glorify Him. Sometimes, it is the struggle itself that truly is the blessing. For that is what can bring us back. That is what can overwhelm and overpower us until there is nothing left for us to do but fall into His arms.

So I say to you today, do not be ashamed. You, too, can repent and turn away from any sin, guilt, or shame you have felt in your life, regardless of whether it was caused by your actions or the actions of others. God can give you strength. We are all broken in some way. Shame cannot withstand the power God gives you when your community in Christ surrounds you. Find your community.

A church elder once told me that you can be fully known and fully loved. I pray that everyone reading this (as well as every one of God's children) can know it is true. You are never alone. God's kingdom is vast, and His eternity is worth any pain we may go through here on this earth. Your shame and your past do not define you. You are a child of God; that is the only label you ever need to put on yourself. Lean into who God has made you to be and the gifts He has given you. Lean into what your struggle has taught you, and let go of any shame you hold onto. You are fully known and fully loved. You are more than your past. I am more than my past. We will meet in His holy kingdom one day, and I can't wait to hug your beautiful soul.

In 1 John 1:9, it says that when we confess our sins, He forgives and purifies us. This means we do not need to let shame and guilt control us. Instead, we can embrace forgiveness and our identity and worth in Christ.

REFLECTIONS:

1. What community do you have in hard times? Do you have Christian brothers/sisters who can offer guidance in strengthening your relationship with God? If so, how do you help each other on your journeys? If not, how can you actively seek out and build that community?
2. What do you know of repentance? How does repentance bring you closer to God?
3. Are there moments in your life that still cause you to feel shame? How can you work toward releasing that shame to God?

Samantha Reimold is a sister in Christ, residing in Staunton, Virginia who, over the past year(ish), has been truly digging into her faith and Scripture and what He wants to be done through her. She has two wild and beautiful children and has been married to her hubby for over eleven years. She and her family recently moved from Virginia Beach to the mountains in Staunton and have found their home there. She has always seen herself as Christian and tried to be a "good human," but she never fully grasped the fullness of God and His goodness and what that meant for her and others. She has been on a faith journey and has had her eyes opened multiple times. So far, this journey has led her to a new home, a new community, and to everyone at F.I.T. Press; she couldn't be more excited.

"Do not be afraid, you will not be put to shame. Do not fear disgrace, you will not be humiliated. You will forget the shame of your youth and remember no more the reproach of your widowhood."

~Isaiah 54:4

CHAPTER 10

Not Ashamed of My Scars

By Marisa Snyder

After losing my husband to a four-year battle with cancer, I found myself in a lost place. I remember looking into the mirror after returning home from the funeral and staring at someone I didn't recognize. I had no idea who I was, let alone who I was supposed to be, as I was forced to embark on this life as a single mom without the man I thought I would spend the rest of my life with.

Realization

As I tried to manage the confusion and lost feelings I was consumed with, I always found peace in the outdoors. I felt God's presence closer to me when I would escape from the busy world and step into the open air, where my focus was on Him. I found that the time I spent hiking, fishing, and hunting allowed me the solitude I needed to recognize and think about who I was and what I enjoyed doing. I stepped out of my comfort zone, trying new things and taking on new adventures. Being outside was my safe place to open myself up to God, but the more time I spent there in God's presence, the more I unconsciously recognized that it was my refuge to open myself up to me.

One early morning, as I watched the sunrise from my porch swing, taking time to self-reflect, God revealed to me an experience I had encountered as a young girl, one which I hid and blocked from my memory due to shame. Reflecting on this event, I was faced with the remembrance of being molested. Hidden emotions I worked so hard to shun surged like a rushing wave, demanding acknowledgment, pulling me into the depths of feelings I could no longer avoid. I was confronted with a challenge that I now had to navigate bravely. I was not ready to face the emotions that had me bound by chains and fear as I sat on that porch swing. Denial immediately set in. I became angry. I questioned why God would allow me to be confronted with this horrible recollection at a time when I was already dealing with so much—navigating the loss of my husband, being a single mom to my daughter, and living a life alone with no one I felt I could turn to or talk to. God was preparing me for my time of healing and redemption. As I gathered my thoughts, the awareness was evident. I was forced to make a conscious effort and recognize that being a victim of molestation was the wound that spiraled and led me into self-destruction and the false manipulation of who I was. So, I simply stood there in God's presence with tears flowing from my eyes.

Layer after layer, God began uncovering every piece of shameful evidence I carried within me. One at a time, these pieces were openly displayed for me to confront: the moments in my life when I felt unworthy of being loved, the times that I convinced myself it wasn't enough just to be me (for fear of being unable to fit in or make anyone happy), and finally moving deeper into the time when they all built upon one another into utter humiliation. This pain consumed every ounce of my being—all my hurt and the destruction that represented who I thought I was looking right at me. I found myself wanting to turn and run away from this harsh reality that I had hidden, but I was paralyzed.

God knew that to fulfill my calling of helping others, He first needed me to find healing within myself.

As I wept, I heard God's gentle voice whisper, "You are more than this. This doesn't define who you are. You are a child of God." This was when I realized that carrying these burdens was beyond what I could handle. I lifted my arms to God and said,

"No more. My past will not have a hold of me any longer." I fell to my knees as the warmth of the morning sun surrounded me. I felt as though God was holding me in His embrace. God knew that to fulfill my calling of helping others, He first needed me to find healing within myself. Just as God spoke to Israel in Isaiah 54:4, offering them assurance of His promise that the shame of their past would be forgotten, so, too, was God beginning to show me that the shame I allowed to humiliate and disgrace me would be forgotten as well.

The Turning Point: I Was Not to Blame for My Shame

Recognizing that my shame didn't define me anymore was easy to claim verbally, but every day called for me to stop and evaluate what I was telling myself. I spent time in God's Word to confirm who Christ created me to be and to speak His truth over myself. I began to learn my identity in Christ and, at the same time, offer healing to the identity that was created from the lies I allowed myself to be defined by in my past. God was molding me to see myself through His lens of biblical truth. Day after day, His words were pressed into my heart. I began to look at my reflection in the mirror and purposefully recognize myself as the one He spoke life into. I had a purpose, and that purpose offered me peace that came from my new relationship with God.

I want to share with you a revelation I encountered as I started my journey of reading the Bible and deepening my understanding of God's Word. I vividly remember holding my Bible close to my chest and asking God, "Where do I even start?" With a quick reply, He said, "At the beginning."

I opened to the Bible's first book, Genesis, and began my quest. As I was reading, I recognized how this book, specifically the story of Adam and Eve, was an excellent example of how the enemy's lies can deceive us into shame. As I continued reading, I found myself relating to Eve. She believed the lies of Satan when she encountered the serpent in the Garden of Eden. He convinced her that she wouldn't die if she ate from the tree of the knowledge of good and evil. Instead, she would become like God, knowing good and evil. The serpent's cunning words swayed Eve, leading her to disobey God's command. This brought Adam and Eve a sense of shame as they realized their nakedness after eating the forbidden fruit. As I made the connection of the deception of Satan in both our lives, I found myself wanting to find out why I felt the way I did.

I encountered a book called *Lies Women Believe and the Truth That Sets Them Free* by Nancy Leigh DeMoss. The book references the reflection of Eve's story. It highlights common lies or misconceptions that women may believe and contrasts them with biblical truths. The author mentions the importance of recognizing how you see and believe God because how we view God will, in turn, be how we view ourselves.

As I read this book, many of the author's words spoke directly to me. It was as if she had reached into my mind, collected all my thoughts, and placed them on the pages of this book. This connection I felt with Eve also seemed to be familiar to others. I remember thinking to myself, "What? I'm not the only one who believes these lies about themselves?" Although it was a sad realization there were others in this world who had encountered these same feelings and believed these terrible lies, I found comfort in knowing that I wasn't alone.

Just like with Eve, the lies that the serpent convinced me were true created my shame and my depiction of unworthiness. As a result, I began to blame myself for what happened to me and further allowed my shame to dictate what I thought of myself. Satan used his cunning words to sway me from God's truth and consume me with his lies. As I clung to this truth, I recognized that not only was I being betrayed by Satan, but I was also betraying and turning against the God who loved me. I had allowed myself to neglect God's truth and only focus on the lies.

As I worked through the chapters of this book, I was able to rebuke Satan's manipulation of my thoughts and replace it with God's truth. Upon completing the book, I found reassurance that I was not to blame for my shame. For thirty years, Satan used his lies to distort my perception and my reality of who I was. It was time to transform my mind and heart as I learned about God's truth. Spending time praying, seeking God's guidance, and equipping my heart with God's truth were my compass that led to the reconciliation of who I was. God showed me that I was created in His image and loved, no matter what my past exposed about me.

Navigating God's Word: Redemption and a New Identity

My healing did not take place overnight. I have to wake up every day and put on the armor of God. I must fill my heart with God's truth and spend time in His Word daily. Just because I accepted God as my Lord and Savior does not mean that the enemy will stop attacking. It is actually quite the opposite. Satan attempts to destroy my relationship with God by distracting me. His efforts are to isolate me and keep me from the God who provides me with truth and unconditional love. There is not a day that goes by when I don't find myself consumed with the tasks of this world. This is Satan's way of manipulating and swaying my focus away from God and into his chaos and destruction. Every second of the day, I make an asserted effort to recognize this and prioritize my time with God before anything else in my life.

Three years after recollecting my past and starting my journey to find my identity, I vividly remember when I stood and looked back at my life. I could clearly see the work God had done in me over the last few years, and this moment of revelation occurred while I was on a safari trip in Africa. I walked around taking photos at sunset. The sky was glowing. I had never witnessed such a spectacular sight. I remember stopping as I raised my face to the sky to take in the beauty before me, and it was then that I felt a warm presence. As I turned, there it was, so radiantly displayed in my mind as though it were painted right before me in the glow of the sunset. The Lord guided me through every moment where He had walked alongside me in my most complex, darkest, and deepest pain and suffering. The shame I once carried from my past no longer defined me. I was filled with confidence in knowing that I didn't stand alone. God walked alongside me every step of the way and was faithful to see me through.

A year ago, I heard the song "Scars" by the band I Am They. This song depicts these moments in my life so perfectly. As I listened to the words, I was instantly taken back to the time in Africa when I stood in the presence of God and looked back at my past. With every word of the song, I could visually recall how God showed me the moments He walked alongside me. And although my story is filled with wounds, just as the song mentions, I, too, wouldn't trade these wounds for anything. I do not hide from that shame anymore. I share it so that others can see the goodness and faithfulness of God. These scars I have will be the stories God will use to bring hope and healing to others who have endured brokenness like mine. Now, every time I hear this song, It serves as a reminder that the brokenness I lived through for so many years was what brought me to my relationship with Christ. It gives me hope for those I know are struggling in their life, that they, too, will be able to one day look back at their hurt and shame and see how their scars will be God's story to share.

Reflecting on this journey of self-awareness and the discovery of my identity in Christ, I go back to how it all started. The loss I endured from the passing of my husband Jason was the stepping stone that would lead me to the path of healing. As I traveled this path, Isaiah 54:4 would comfort and guide me. "Do not be afraid; you will not be put to shame. Do not fear disgrace; you will not be humiliated. You will forget the shame of your youth and remember no more the reproach of your widowhood."

This verse assures us that we should not fear shame, disgrace, or humiliation. God promises that the shame of our past, represented as our youth and widowhood, will be forgotten. We can find assurance in this verse, as it symbolizes the idea of God's redemption and restoration in our lives, bringing us a brighter future without the burden of past shame and reproach.

As I consider the meaning of this verse as it applies to my circumstances and my life, I find assurance in knowing that the shame, disgrace, and humiliation of being molested as a young girl has been forgotten. . . .

The *shame* of believing that I was to blame is gone.

The *disgrace* of believing I was unworthy of being loved and accepted has been cleared.

The *humiliation* of being judged by others, if they knew the pain that I endured, has been taken from me.

I further reflect on the promise that as God uses me to tell my story and offer hope and healing to others, I do not have to be afraid. My story will not be used as a means of shame or humiliation, for God will use my story for His Glory, as it aids in the acceptance and healing of those who are still bound by chains of shame, hurt, and despair.

Where are you struggling, friend? What lies from your past have a hold on you, keeping you from a life filled with God's peace, joy, and love? Know that you are not alone in your struggle. Rest assured that the God that brought you into the world is the same God waiting for you to extend your arms up to Him and declare, "I am yours, Lord. Break these chains that confine me and restrict me from living my life filled with your glory." He longs for you to trust in Him as He walks alongside you into a life filled with hope and healing.

My self-reflection and time with God were crucial to finding my identity in Christ. Allowing myself the time to spend in His presence and hear Him speak the truth about

> **He longs for you to trust in Him as He walks alongside you into a life filled with hope and healing.**

who He created me to be was the essential part of learning who I was. I gained confirmation as God led me through His Word and guided me to verses that spoke of hope, healing, and renewing.

As you begin letting go of how your past has defined you, I encourage you to take time with God and hear Him speak His biblical truths over you. Take time to pray and ask God for clarity as you work together to reveal the beautiful person He created you to be.

Closing Thoughts

If you had asked me five years ago where I thought I would be in my life today, the answer you would have received would look nothing like the reality of the life I am currently living. If God had not allowed me to endure the pain and suffering of my past, I wouldn't have had the opportunity to find my identity in Christ and follow the calling He has placed on my life. I have grown so much from the person I was for many years. The words *hope* and *healing* has taken on new meaning as I look at myself in the mirror now and see a beautiful child of God filled with joy, love, happiness, and, most importantly, peace.

As you stop and think about where you see yourself in five years, consider the trials you have endured. Reflect on how God will use those to create in you the understanding of who He created you to be. Will you listen to His voice and become a new creation in Christ, or will you remain in a place of hiding, a place in your past that you continually allow to define you? I encourage you to take time to deepen your faith and your understanding of your relationship with Christ. I chose to listen to His voice. My prayer is that you will choose that as well.

REFLECTIONS:

Use the following questions as a starting point to help you recognize and evaluate where you are so that God can meet you there. Focus your answers on how you see God's promise for yourself.

1. In what ways can faith and trust in God help you move beyond shame and find a fresh start?
2. What steps can you take to embrace the hope of a future without the burden of shame and reproach?

Marisa Snyder is an author, Christian speaker, life coach, and podcaster. She resides in Texas with her husband and two children. After losing her late husband to cancer, she experienced firsthand the hardship that comes from walking through difficult daily struggles alone. As she moved through this challenging season, she began recognizing her strength, finding her new identity in Christ, and walking by faith into her calling in life. Today, she witnesses the trials that others go through, whether death, divorce, the loss of a job, or the loss of oneself, and she has made it her mission to help them see their strengths, become confident in their journey, recognize who they are in Christ, and deepen their relationship with Him. Her recently launched podcast, website, and social media platforms, *Be Inspired God's Way*, allow her to reach more people with her daily devotionals, blogs, podcasts, and online life coaching.

More THAN My Job

"Then he said, 'Go into the world. Go everywhere and announce the Message of God's good news to one and all. Whoever believes and is baptized is saved, whoever refuses to believe is damned.'"

~Mark 16:15, MSG

CHAPTER 11

Seen Six Feet Under

By Tamra Andress

I launched eight companies in my twenties—most of which flopped, thanks to fads or lack of focus, but I still did it. I've worked for a Fortune 500 company and quickly became recognized by the CEO for ingenuity and excellence. I owned a brick-and-mortar and e-commerce business for five-plus years before I sold it and then helped sell it again. I have signed a seven-figure contract with potential earnings upwards of nine figures as the CEO and designer with global reach and connections worldwide.

This was it, right?

This was the "American Dream."

This was the point of success that most never reached, even with tenure and retirement.

But one unexpected, bleak day, I saw the image of my tombstone staring at me, and it didn't say, *entrepreneur*. I was shocked. I felt void. I went from something to nothing in an instant. And it wasn't solely because my "successes" and accolades weren't listed on the stone that had me shaken; it was because my other "jobs" as wife and mom weren't listed either. But, saddest of all, neither was the common Christian gravestone inscription "Child of God."

I was nothing. This was my quarter-life crisis. At twenty-nine, I didn't have a business card any longer. My name wasn't worthy to be etched into anything. And the "jobs" I did have, the jobs of wife and mom, I imagined away in the dark chasms of my thoughts and circling nightmares.

I wanted out of this cyclone and off this hamster wheel. This was habitual. This was ingrained. This was trauma-induced. This was societally the norm. This was what reality shows, commercials, and magazines created. This was what I was in debt for since college. This was what a shiny name tag and 401k got me. This was what accolades and labor-intensive leadership created. This was what expectations dictated for me to do. This was what my signature led to. This was life as I knew it. This was my job. And now it had become my gravesite. But simply stopping, even with an eviction notice brought on by my lack of integrity in those "hot shot" roles, didn't ease the fatigue or pain. I still had to face the tombstone.

The good news is I did surrender. I lifted my white flag, and I tucked my tail between my legs, as they say, and I called it **all** quits—mainly in order to regain some sense of ego, normalcy, and peace beyond the shame and unhealthy cycles. But despite surrendering, I still thought I could "work" my way out of this pit I had dug six feet under. After all, I had released the jobs and picked up therapy in order to be a better wife and human, and I had become a stay-at-home mom . . . my newest title.

I found, however, that I didn't know how to rest. I didn't know how to communicate deeply with others. I didn't know how to read or dissect my own emotions. I didn't know what to do with "downtime." I didn't know how to process my pains. I discovered; even with *all* the job titles, roles, responsibilities, accomplishments, and beyond; I had no idea what my passion was and was wildly removed from my purpose—I needed purpose in this new plan. I needed a strategy to cope. I needed to "launch" something. And what I found was a way of life I had never experienced before.

Now, I didn't come to this revelation easily. Instead, it came to me through a radical encounter with Jesus. At this point in my life, I was a "chriseaster" (a.k.a. a Christmas and Easter Christian). I didn't attend church. I didn't listen to worship music. I didn't know God at all; in fact, I just knew about Him. Until . . . He decided to make himself known and become unignorable. This was a reckless pursuit. This was success, as I had never known, because it was full of sustenance. This was a title I had never held, and I didn't have to work for it. He had already done the work on the cross. I surrendered. Again.

> He decided to make himself known and become unignorable.

But surrender is simply releasing the reigns, which is not the same as submission. Surrender is letting someone else win, while submission is honoring the one who won it all. I realized that surrendering wasn't enough . . . I would have to submit. To bow down. To take my eyes off me, my problems, and my endless pursuit of an impossible personal perfection so that I could stare perfection in the face.

Within weeks of meeting God in my living room, where He spoke to me directly, I wanted nothing more than to chase after Him. (You can find out what He said and more about that encounter in my book *Always Becoming: Sex, Shame & Love*.) Through worship, the Word, and warfare, the desires of the world started to fade, and a new sense of identity started to emerge. I had been released from the enemy's camp, but all of the grit and grind I had developed throughout my childhood and young adult years weren't wasted at all when I started to pursue His presence. This wasn't my job. This was my calling. He is my calling.

Now, this might seem like a big gap, but death to life happened in a three-day span for Jesus—and we serve a supernatural God—so why not me? Why not you? I get it, though. You want the details. The timeline. The **how**. (Again, read my other book . . . this is about **you,** not me.) I'm clearly not God, and my wounds did need deep healing and mending. I needed time to unlearn so I could relearn. I needed to re-establish my life on a firm foundation rather than on the quicksand society presented as a life fixated on vacation. Work hard. Play hard. Right?

Wrong.

Very, very wrong.

Over the course of the next several years, I filled in the burial site I had previously dug, and I planted a garden that now bears much fruit. And as people come to visit it, read the inscription, and connect with who I am and was, that tombstone, the one I will one day revisit, has become a place of life and not death—this time with Truth-telling titles and jobs that make me proud.

So that's me . . . but what about her; more importantly, what about you?

This is a devotional intended to impact women. And this story, while mine, may not meet you. But I'm wise enough now to know that there are layers to the experiences you have encountered within your job(s). Layers that you might have never dissected—ways you've been pushed down, quieted, sexualized, dismissed, passed by, demoted, undervalued, criticized, and perhaps even championed (of course, for their gain whether you knew it at the time or not).

You see, I have those stories too. We still operate in a man's world. I remember one moment in particular when I no longer had titles or current successes to share and was attending an event with my husband—it was a moment of shame. I used to be able to handle the guys in suits, but this time, when I shared that I was a stay-at-home mom and studying to be an ordained minister, I was met with crickets and quick distractions. These types of reactions became commonplace in conversations that used to carry "what's in it for me" undertones of curiosity. Even in my faith journey as an entrepreneur operating as a marketplace minister in the business coaching arena, I've felt these icky moments of tension, moments where I have been marginalized, sexualized, or had my voice diminished—moments where I have been taken advantage of. But I no longer seek to have the right answers or to correct their wrong ideas of my worth. Now, I run to His Truth to teach me and define me rather than letting my mind (which can be a battlefield) make up stories of whether I'm "good or bad" at my job.

Let's consider the women of the Word and how we can fully relate to them despite the seemingly different times we live in (Ecclesiastes 1:9). Let's analyze our similarities and define our differences—making way for the Holy Spirit to show us where we may be sharpened and made mature so as to become the pure bride we are destined to be (Ephesians 5:27), not by works but by faith (Ephesians 2:8–9).

Think of Esther in this scenario . . . how she must have felt being plucked out and brought to the palace to become something she wasn't for someone she didn't love or know. She was coined by her job as queen and used for her body and beauty, yet her wisdom became an underlying current for Christ. Her placement and position were used for a mighty purpose. And ours can be too. But that does not mean we must jeopardize ourselves to fit a role, a financial need, or a facade of what we think we need to be in order to be successful, important, or worthy.

Think of Ruth. She was willing to show up as a poor beggar in the fields of Boaz, collecting the leftovers of his workers. Because she honored God and her mother-in-law, she was favored and was provided abundance and, ultimately found safety, love, and provision. You don't have to be the owner of the field or the boss lady. You can serve and be seen too.

Think of Martha. She caught God's attention by questioning her sister's perceived laziness because she was a natural "doer." Can you relate? Clearly, I can. I love Martha so much, and I value that she was the first to go out to meet Jesus when her brother Lazarus had been dead in his grave for days. Though she may have used an accusatory tone with Jesus, she had devout faith in His healing power, and Jesus proved her "faith-full" when He raised Lazarus from the tomb.

We all have different sides to who we are. Martha was speculative, fiery, and focused, perhaps not always on the right things, but she did love and honor Jesus. Similarly, in my own life, there was a "Mary" way of loving and leaning in that I didn't readily adopt until I understood how to rest in Him—learning that my identity was at His feet, not in busying myself for Him.

Think of Deborah—the only female judge and only one of five female prophets mentioned in the Old Testament. She was a woman of wisdom. And even with all of her roles (poet, warrior, singer, and songwriter), she was remembered because of her relationship with God. He spoke to her, and she responded despite the traditional masculine and feminine roles of that day. She was courageous, and she obeyed. As women in the workforce, the home, the community, and society at large, we all need to carry the Deborah anointing—to listen and stand up despite our fears or common practices.

And then there's Mary. Her proximity and eagerness to be ever closer to Christ inspires me. She was willing to wash His feet as her "job" and prepare His body for the tomb, not because she was asked but because she loved Him. (See this chapter's resources for a blog that discusses whether Mary of Bethany and Mary Magdalene are one and the same.) She was willing to pause every earthly, fleshly calling to be within His call and presence. She was there to witness His rise, His fall, and His resurrection. She did what I hope to do as well: exude excellence and presence in all the things the Lord has called me to do with my gifts and talents . . . to dwell well.[1]

If we can place emphasis on the practice of dwelling, a practice that all of these women possessed in one way or another, it will shine a light on our purpose and release us from our "duties." And though we have responsibilities, and the pursuit and practice of our faith are fundamental to our growth and service here on Earth (as it is in heaven), we don't have to follow the ways of the world to be recognized by the world. In fact, because we will be known by our fruit (Matthew 7:15–20) and know God as the ultimate gardener, our practice of dwelling becomes all the more

---

1 Butz, Jeffrey. "Was Mary Magdalene the Same Person as Mary of Bethany?" TaborBlog by Dr. James Tabor, Oct. 10, 2020, https://jamestabor.com/was-mary-magdalene-the-same-person-as-mary-of-bethany-a-guest-post-from-jeffrey-butz/.

critical—as He is the lifespring that nurtures, grows, and generates plenty for multiplication.

Today, we still speak about these women. They have names that have endured for centuries and will continue to be voiced into eternity. You have a book He has authored as well. A story that's being written. A story that is not defined by your earthly roles or paychecks or business cards. It is a story meant to be told because

You have a book He has authored as well. A story that's being written.

it's meant to proclaim the one who breathed you into being—long before you ever got hired to be something you were never meant to become.

There is one thing I know for certain: you were meant to Go and Tell the World (Mark 16:15). No matter your position. No matter your place. No matter your present circumstance. You were made to activate—to Go. And, as women, we've always been good at this second part—to Tell.

Perhaps you're ready to start writing (or speaking) your story for others, being the brave one, the bold one, the one who releases a sound uniquely yours. I have a heart for developing messengers because, ultimately, that's what we're here to do—together. This is the body of Christ operating with our diverse sounds, tunes, and rhythms that will one day make up the shared sound of heaven's choir.

While my previous jobs did *not* include any of that in their descriptions, I have so loved watching God use every area of development, every past role, responsibility, and learned lesson to meld, redesign, and establish my new "job," if that's what you want to call it. This is what I get to do, not what I have to do. But it *is* like Mary, what I'm called to do. My whole being leans into it all night long in my dreams, in my prayers, and from the moment my feet hit the ground. I don't punch a time clock. No one pays me a salary. No day is an "off day," and I don't work for a weekend or dread a Monday. I don't answer to a boss, but I do submit to the King.

I'm not fixated on success anymore because I've tasted and seen that the Lord is far more fulfilling and much richer than any job title or contract could offer me. He's resourced beyond my wildest imaginations, and He has never once asked me to do anything that would step out of alignment with my identity and His great love for me as His child.

And guess what?

My job doesn't differ from yours or hers or his. Ultimately, as disciples, we all get to do the same thing, to share the good news just as the woman at the well did when she was radically changed because she was radically seen! And I'll never forget the moment I was seen—outside of a job, inside of a role—as daughter.

So, while each of us has jobs . . . the J-O-B is not what defines you. And what you can give or get on this side of heaven won't follow you to the grave or be with you in eternity. So why not stay diligent about the One who never takes His eyes off you? The One who calls you daughter. The One who calls you worthy. The One who calls you worth it. The One who calls you woman.

You and I are not our jobs. We are His daughters. So stop trying so hard to be seen; He is the One who sees you (Genesis 16:13).

REFLECTIONS:

1. Where are you striving when it comes to your job, and what areas within that job are not fully aligned to your Kingdom calling or mission?
2. Scripturally, who do you need to learn from in this season of responsibility and seeking?
3. How is God sweetly summoning and convicting you to become His messenger right now? And what can you do today to Go and activate and Tell?

Tamra Andress is a six-time #1 best-selling author (and counting . . .), a passionate top 1 percent global podcaster (*The Messenger Movement Podcast, Girls Gone Holy Podcast & The Founder Collective Podcast*), an international speaker, Kingdom messenger & experience creator with retreats and events. She's the founder of F.I.T. In Faith Media & Press Christian Publishing House. She serves as the president of The Founder Collective, a non-profit with a mobilized church for entrepreneurs, birthing an academy of marketplace ministers. All of her initiatives are centralized to catalyze faith-filled leaders into messengers with movements so that they can broadcast Truth and advance the kingdom.

"A wise woman builds her home, but a foolish woman tears it down with her own hands."

~Proverbs 14:1, NLT

CHAPTER 12

The Role that Defines Me

By Victoria Ciresi

It's 11:35 p.m., and I have been up since 4:00 a.m. I am halfway through the work week and already logged forty-one hours. Tonight, my family had dinner on their own. My kiddos have fallen asleep on the sofa, and my husband went to bed a few hours ago. I am still sitting in front of my laptop with so many open items, feeling overwhelmed and anxious, knowing the day starts over again tomorrow at 4:00 a.m.

As with each of us, there are a lot of layers. I'm a mama of three fellas and a wife of seventeen years. I've been a business owner and worked in the corporate world, but I currently serve as an executive leader for a women's boutique fitness franchise. And as you'll learn, I'm a "more is never enough" type of individual.

I grew up in church and believed in God for as long as I can remember, but it wasn't until a rainy Friday night, a few weeks after my twenty-second birthday, that I surrendered my life to Jesus. This chapter doesn't share much of my "at the cross" moment, but it will provide a deep dive into my continual need to surrender my heart to God, especially as it relates to one particular area of my life . . .

As I sit here and pray and try to write these words, I realize how difficult it is for us to share our vulnerabilities and insecurities and speak the truth. But here goes . . . I find it highly challenging to fully surrender one area of my life to God—my job! The Lord has been evident in each step of my working journey, but I often lose sight of Him and try to take the reins. Through fear (not of the Lord), I become prideful, controlling, and stubborn. Throughout my journey, I've often gotten lost in the world's view of what success looks like and falsely determined my worth in what I do each day. My identity became how well I performed, often through monetary gains, a title, or more responsibility. Success for me, from the world's perspective, was never enough. God has shown me a lot over the last few years. Who am I serving? Why am I serving? How am I serving? It wasn't until recently that I realized I was entirely misaligned from Christ; my well was dry, and there was little fruit. My story today will share the journey I have been on to find my true role, the role that has always defined me.

Let's begin by looking at our anchor verse from Proverbs. This verse states, "A wise woman builds her home, but a foolish woman tears it down with her own hands" (Proverbs 14:1, NLT). When I read these words, I see a beautiful depiction of a woman's heart posture through her hands. Like the wise woman in the Scripture, our heart posture should be one of connection with God. And as I reflect on how the wise woman's hands are positioned, I see them being open, facing up to the Lord. When our hands are in this position, we can receive and serve others. When I think of the foolish woman in this Scripture, her heart posture is misaligned with God. We are told she is tearing her home down with her hands. I picture balled-up fists that are closed, tight, and maybe even knocking down what the Lord has built up for her. When I read this verse a few years ago, it hit deep. I'd been that foolish woman, needing constant refinement, redirection, and repurposing so my heart and hands could remain open. There is so much freedom in having a surrendered heart with open hands to serve, and I can't wait to share how this has advanced my walk with Jesus and created healing and fruit in my family! I want us to unpack three areas related to our heart posture: *motivation*, *priorities*, and *counsel*.

Before we dive into the three areas, I'd love to share how my career journey started. I'm number four out of nine children. Through my self-awareness, I believe a lot of my internal wiring stems from being a part of such a large family. My working journey started with a pair of Nikes. I made the basketball team during my freshman year in high school. This was exciting, but I needed basketball shoes, and I didn't want to be the only player without the "good" shoes—I wanted Jordans. With such a large family, money was tight. With older siblings, I often received hand-me-downs; the drawback was that my older siblings were much smaller than me, and often, the items didn't fit. I remember the overwhelming feelings of angst when I asked my dad for the money to buy the shoes. Looking back, a few needs that were evident during that moment in my life.

First and foremost, I had a need for harmony, especially with my family. I also uncovered needs for affirmation, fitting in, and connection with my teammates (that I thought the Jordans would provide me). Ultimately, I chose the needs related to my teammates' image of me, and my dad bought me the shoes. I immediately felt shame. I told myself that day I'd never ask for money again, and the next week, fifteen years old, I started my first job at a local restaurant. This ignited an insatiable desire to earn money and control my way through the world. By the time I was nineteen, I had three jobs while still attending school.

What I've shared so far is just a small portion of how I was propelled into the working world at an early age. These early jobs provided skills like work ethic, time and money management, and sociability. They also taught me to perform at a high level and identify behaviors that would translate into success. I learned that if you want something, just work hard and keep putting in more reps. What I didn't expect was that my work would become such a source of significance and create an often unhealthy ambition with my controlling desire to provide for my unmet needs. You see, the culture of this world will tell you that success equals more. Wanting more. Doing more. Having more. And I listened to the world, claiming *its* truth as my own—"more is never enough."

I believe God gifts us with experiences (good and bad), strengths, and abilities that are to be used with excellence for whatever He calls us to through faith, but it's for His glory and not our own. I also believe when we try to control the outcomes due to our sinful nature (mainly brought on by fear), we lose out on the true blessings and fruit that He has for us. When I think back on the two women in Proverbs 14:1, I feel burdened that I continued to carry the heart posture of the foolish woman throughout my working journey, and you'll see this through the three areas we will break down—*motivations, priorities,* and *counsel.* I encourage you to assess your heart in these areas as we move forward.

Let's talk about Paul. I'm a huge fan! His incredible salvation story and his complete redirection of his life are honorable. I also respect the leadership he provided the church. He reminds us constantly through his writings that no matter where we are called to give our time, talent, and treasure, God is calling us to be "steadfast, immovable, always abounding in the work of the Lord, knowing that [our] labor is not in vain for the Lord" (1 Corinthians 15:58, NKJV).

A wise woman works for the Lord and is motivated by kingdom glory.

Paul reminds us that our mission is for the kingdom, and whatever gifts we've been given by the Lord or station we've been called to will not be used in vain if it's for Jesus.

A wise woman works for the Lord and is *motivated* by kingdom glory. Times when I've forgotten my identity as a believer, and my heart posture was misaligned with God were the times when I prioritized the mission of the business I was serving above God's mission. Success from the world's view provided profitable businesses but left me empty, burnt out, and completely overwhelmed. I became primarily motivated by money, influence, and worldly praise. As a remote business owner in 2017, I remember prioritizing the mission of my personal business above the mission God had for me and my family. I was afraid of failure in the business, and somewhere along the lines, I stopped fully trusting that He was in control. I prioritized relationships with my members above my own family, and when I was home, I was not fully present with my husband or children. I had fear, real fear, that if I weren't in the business all the time, we wouldn't be successful. As a result, I spent a lot of time traveling. I had similar experiences working in the corporate world.

Colossians 3:23–24, Paul writes, "Whatever you do, work at it with all your heart, as working for the Lord, not for human masters, since you know that you will receive an inheritance from the Lord as a reward. It's the Lord Christ you are serving." This verse encourages us to approach our work and daily tasks with dedication and wholeheartedness, seeing our efforts as a way to serve the Lord and not just our earthly employers, businesses, or ourselves (families). It reminds us that our ultimate reward comes from serving God faithfully in all we do. At a conference recently, I heard a worship leader speak about letting everything you do be a form of worship. Wow, that's powerful. Think about this when kissing your kiddos goodbye on their way to school, typing an email to a colleague, or preparing a meal for your family. . . . Everything we do is for the Lord! Paul again reminds us in Colossians that our mission is for the kingdom. What does kingdom work look like, and where is your heart? The culture we live in today promotes the more-is-never-enough mentality. I'm here to share that the wise woman is motivated by and living for the kingdom's mission. She may never fully know the impact of her labor, but by living in His will, there will be fruit in her life due to her surrendered heart and serving hands.

What we truly value (our *priorities*) will drive our behaviors, and this is magnified when we face adversity. I don't want you to miss this point, so I will share it again—*our real priorities will become magnified when we face adversity.* One of my favorite passages in the Bible is in Jeremiah. It states, "But blessed is the one who trusts in the Lord, whose confidence is in Him. They will be like a tree planted by the water that sends out its roots by the stream. It does not fear when heat comes; its leaves are always green. It has no worries in a year of drought and never fails to bear fruit" (Jeremiah 17:7–8).

A wise woman *prioritizes* the Lord and His kingdom above the world. With my more-is-never-enough attitude, I intentionally come back to this verse to consider a few things in light of Jeremiah 17: am I truly trusting God in the outcomes, and when faced with adversity, what is my heart posture, faith, or fear? I am wildly aware that apart from Him, I try to control outcomes. I learned early on that through hard work and my ambition, I could be successful, but in those seasons, I became overwhelmed and empty, and the fruit was limited. My soul was thirsty. To be fully transparent, my self-defined identity became skewed from His truth. This is when the world's culture creeps in, and we forget the importance of surrendering our faith and heart to Him.

I remember distinctly feeling empty, broken and misaligned throughout the pandemic. This is true for many, but for me, most of it resulted from where I placed my value. When the world began shutting down, this high-A, more-is-never-enough individual prioritized her life in the following order: my job, my children, my husband, and then God. While I was in the midst of it all, I was unaware, almost in fight mode, but I was fighting with the wrong weapons. I stopped praying, began drinking daily, and was connected to work 24/7. I lived with the fear of not being good enough for my employer, fear of being unable to lead through adversity, and not showing the courage to do the hard things (like still showing up despite being completely overwhelmed). It took almost two years to realize the magnitude of this misalignment. And this was the first time I feared for my marriage.

For our first thirteen years together, we had a rhythm that worked for us but one that we could no longer live out each day. My husband was working from home while I was still going into the office. Our prior routine shifted, and both of us had to step into new roles that were somewhat foreign. With this sudden shift of roles on the home front, we hit an obstacle we had never dealt with, and the depths of my heart were revealed. After intense fellowship with my husband and months of conversations, the Holy Spirit convicted me to surrender my heart. If our behaviors are driven by motives that are anything other than Jesus first, our hearts will be misaligned. Through prayer and time in God's Word, I could see no fruit in any area of my life.

I have shared the word *fruit* several times, but I want to make sure we pause and consider what that means. It's mentioned in Jeremiah 17:7–8, and Paul references the "fruit of the Spirit" in Galatians 5:22–23. "But the fruit of the Spirit is love, joy, peace, forbearance, kindness, goodness, faithfulness, gentleness, and self-control." I believe the wise woman would have evidence of fruit in her life. I assessed my heart against these fruits, and it was empty. I was not living in alignment with the way the Lord called me to and was destroying my family unit. My identity had to be reclaimed in Jesus and not placed in my role at work. Remembering the wise woman, the Bible tells us that "she *builds* her home" (Proverbs 14:1, NLT). So, my role as a believer starts with investing in my home, and my priorities become God first, followed by my husband, my children, and *then* my work.

In a world full of influencers and with content so freely at our fingertips, it's easy to be misled on truth. But Proverbs 4:23 tells us to "guard [our] heart for everything [we] do flows from it." I believe a wise woman will seek godly *counsel*. Are we seeking God's wisdom and affirmation first or the world's? Are we always the light in a dark place or fellowshipping only with other believers? Who are we "doing life" with, and what is their heart posture?

To stay focused on the wise woman from Proverbs 14:1, we should remember that she is *building* up her home. That starts with seeking godly wisdom. For me, it's picking **The wisest thing we can do is connect with God first, before anyone else.** the Bible up first thing in the morning. It's praying before seeking advice from others. And it's finding time in stillness and silence. I recently read a book by Wendy Blight titled *Rest For Your Soul*, and wow, the Lord spoke to me through Wendy's heart. I needed discernment and felt stuck; she shared that to hear from God, especially in a world with so much noise, it was important to find time alone in silence. But even in that silence, could I truly discern God's voice from the world's voice? Yes! Discernment comes through Scripture reading and, more importantly, Scripture memorization! Psalm 119:11 shares, "I have hidden your word in my heart that I might not sin against you." Admittedly, It's difficult at times to discern the voice of God above others, but those are the times we must turn to the Scriptures. When I start having unpleasant feelings, such as anxiety, depression, or fear, I'm immediately reminded of the truth of God's Word. Isaiah 26:3 says, "You will keep in perfect peace those whose minds are steadfast because they trust in you." His Word always brings me comfort and provides direction.

The wisest thing we can do is connect with God first, before anyone else. Proverbs 15:33 tells us that "wisdom's instruction is to fear the Lord, and humility comes before honor." This verse instructs us that true wisdom starts with a deep reverence for the Lord and that we should first exhibit humility and respect toward God and others before receiving honor or recognition. By doing so, He will fill our needs to be seen, heard, and valued. And ultimately, He will guide our steps. When we acknowledge our limitations and our total dependence on Him, it will always lead to greater rewards for the kingdom.

I had the privilege of hearing Christian author and entrepreneur Stephen Scoggins speak this year. He had so many nuggets of godly wisdom, but my favorite was the last thing he shared: "We should all be one part *lion* and one part *lamb*." I'm unsure if this was his original thought, but I'm thankful for his sharing. I often joke with my husband that I'm a lion and God created me to hunt. God has gifted each of us uniquely, and as Stephen's quote reminded me, as long as we take the *Lamb* with us in everything we do, we can use our gifts for kingdom glory.

The Lord has this uncanny way of sending the Holy Spirit to speak to me at two and three a.m. It's a nudge to get me up just a little earlier to spend time with Him or His way of telling me something really important. Sometimes, it takes a few days to discern the message; most often, it's the answer to something I've been praying over. "More than enough. More than enough. More than enough." At two o'clock in the morning, forty-eight hours ago, I heard this from the Lord. There was no other call to action . . . just these words repeated for almost an hour. I'd been praying over this chapter for what seemed like weeks, and I knew I wanted to share in a way that glorified the Lord. I was scrambled in my head, heavy in my heart, uneasy in my soul, and I didn't know where to begin, how I would end, or what was most important to share. His words to me were a reminder that there is no need to get up and "do" right now. You are "more than enough," and He has this! He knows He created me to be a lion, but His reminder was not to forget the Lamb!

Today, forty-eight hours later, I've surrendered to where I know He's called me to share, and though I've forever had the motto of More is Never Enough, I am called to tell you that *He is enough*, and I have reclaimed my identity and the role that truly defines me—Believer in Christ Jesus! The sacrifice Jesus made on the cross is where we find we are "More Than" in Him. The work's been done; we just need to surrender our hearts (and jobs) with open hands like the wise woman!

REFLECTIONS:

1. What areas of your life are you holding onto that you need to surrender to God?
2. How are you prioritizing your day?
3. Lastly, who are you surrounding yourself with, and are they pointing you back to Christ?

Victoria Ciresi, born and raised in Maryland, currently resides in Denver, North Carolina, with her husband, three sons, two dogs, and ten chickens. She was raised in a large family of nine children, with two brothers and six sisters. At the age of twenty-two, she dedicated her life to Jesus. With a passion for writing and a compassionate dedication to ministry, she runs Casa Gioiosa (Joyful Home), where she lovingly prays for and prepares and delivers meals to those in need. Victoria also works outside the home, serving as the vice president of culture for a rapidly expanding fitness franchise. She has extensive experience in business management, leadership, and HR and currently leads the people strategy for the organization. With her life experiences, leadership in a women-focused organization, and six sisters, she has a heart for ministering to women to find their true identity in Jesus.

More THAN a Wife

"Am I now trying to win the approval of human beings, or of God? Or am I trying to please people? If I were still trying to please people, I would not be a servant of Christ."

~Galatians 1:10

CHAPTER 13

More Than a Pastor's Wife: Riding the Waves

By Sandra Coates

The Undertow

As daybreak opened and the sky announced it was light, I walked up to the sand. Seagulls were flying, and sets of waves were coming in. I felt the excitement of escaping for a morning surf session.

Living by the ocean means you get to experience the grandeur and beauty of God's creation, the sea. It's a beautiful playground for us all to enjoy and take refuge in. But it also means you must prepare for the storms that come when the weather takes a turn. When the winds whip and the ocean's roar feels angry, you catch a glimpse of its true power and force. Your home must be built to withstand those high winds and the potential destruction that can result. It is not forgiving nor a respecter of persons. The ocean tides ebb and flow depending on forces outside of your control. It never stops.

Similarly, I thought that by maturing as a woman of God, I would be trained and ready when unexpected events happened. Being one who was excited to be all in as God's warrior meant I would never get burned out or want to get out. And I would certainly not be rocked by my insecurities and shame over who I saw when I looked in the mirror. I had prayed so hard and saw God do miracles as I stood by my husband and watched his life become his vocation. Wasn't that enough? Why couldn't I just stop all the aches and be grateful and happy for what I had been given? But instead, I had learned to be a chameleon.

The real me was buried inside. I didn't feel I was enough, just as I was. I was supposed to fill this role of caring, investing in others' lives, and knowing what to say and how to pray. I expected myself to have a certain gift mix. Isn't that what a "good" pastor's wife has? Isn't she the one who offers godly wisdom and guidance and radiates joy and compassion without pause?

In a world filled with surface hellos, likes, and quick-heart emojis, finding the authentic and "real you" within a community is not an easy task. The millions of thoughts, emotions, stressors, and decisions that each of us experiences in a day or a season often put us outside of our capacity. And we know we can easily take on too much in a day—most days if we are honest. We all wear many different hats and can easily be hit with situations outside of our scope. Unfortunately, it has become the norm to live this way,

Where are the rhythms of me amid the scripts that lure me into putting on titles that pull me away from realizing who I am, even before I start?

so we often don't know why we can't shake the labels we place on ourselves (like "so busy," "just trying to keep up," or "not being so stressed"). If I had a dollar for every time one of these phrases came out of my mouth, all of you would join me on an all-expenses-paid dream vacation!

So, who am I becoming amid the hyperstimulated world around me, a world that includes silent, lonely parts mixed with fast-paced demands and high expectations? Where are the rhythms of me amid the scripts that lure me into putting on titles that pull me away from realizing who I am, even before I start? None of us set out to achieve goals or schedules that are harmful or meaningless in the end. But who we are and who we serve, apart from the noise or the applause or the pressures, will set the course for where our focus is and impact our ability to attain our goals instead of being trampled by them.

As I prepare for Sunday church, I think of many things. Sometimes, it is a burden for a person or a situation that lies heavy on my heart or a relationship that is in conflict with the leadership. Sometimes, it is the excitement of wondering who God will have me talk with today or the word I will receive in service from Him. And sometimes, it's just plain anxiety or numbness, asking God to intercede during a difficult period. As we walk into the busy foyer, with the hustle of people talking, greeting one another, and congregating near the coffee station, I prepare to smile and engage. The role in my head feels normal, even though my life events from the past week are different and often overwhelming. Some mornings, I am excited to be there, and other mornings, I don't feel I have anything to give. On those days, it feels easier to hide.

Navigating a church's culture and investing in close relationships with people is wonderful. Being intimately involved in other people's lives allows for deep, God-centered friendships that feel more like family than work. And although it is not automatic or even guaranteed, when it happens, life is brought to your soul.

But while I try my best to balance being vulnerable and available with assertiveness and confidence, I experience both the calm and the stormy encounters. What do I mean by that? Well, sometimes, being in this role is exhausting and full of deep hurt and pain as I walk through other people's sadness and betrayal. In my position, I risk getting hurt and hurting others I care about. But I don't get to clock in or out of this role; it is a job without a job description.

So, I find a balance between the different circles of people and their ideas of what my titles represent and who my husband is. At times, my motives or personal life can be questioned simply because of the title I bear, the events I attend, and the friendships I hold. And what happens when I make a mistake or say something wrong? Is there room to forgive others or to be forgiven?

But, at the end of the day, witnessing God's miracles in the lives of others is truly an amazing assignment! To stand by my husband in his calling as a pastor and watch him pour himself into the church body is an incredible, faith-growing opportunity. As I have traveled with him on this journey, there have been some seasons where I have been very involved and others where I have been barely visible. During some of those times of "invisibility," my family needed me to hold things together, or my children simply needed me to be present with them. At other times, I simply carried the weight of wanting to be part of the church while not always knowing how.

As for Me

To know me is to know I love fashion. Equipping other females to see their beauty and value is in my blood. But first, I had to walk out my own testimony. Fashion always seemed to help mask the wounded parts and soften the blows of the relentless questioning about my age, my weight, or what grade I was really in. Underneath it all, when I looked at myself in the mirror, I longed to be someone else. I craved confidence but instead carried an insecure body image and a ruthless inner critic. Since I was a girl, I agonized over my size and often felt I was too big. It felt like a disease or disability that I was forced to live with, and I didn't think that God cared enough to fix it. What I didn't know was that He wanted to use the very thing I was begging Him to change as a backdrop for the grand story He was writing within me. I was not forgotten. He had a plan all along.

> **He wanted me to use the very thing I was begging Him to change as a backdrop for the grand story He was writing within me.**

Every single one of us has a uniqueness about us. We are not copycats of each other, nor are we meant to be. We are originals—masterpieces—that God designed to stand out and be used as an instrument to relate to others. Not one is better or more successful. But instead, your story, style, and gifting show His unlimited creativity and beauty. We are all made up of different personalities fueled by different things (surrounding our calling to be a servant of Christ), and we have specific life stories that funnel and shape who we are and how we engage with those around us.

I eventually realized that I had to come to the end of myself. And to do that, I had to allow God to rewrite my self-worth and identity. This wasn't a quick process, however. It took me a long time to find who I was apart from the roles I played. I had torn myself down and made false idols out of achievements and lifelines out of compliments. I had to take a risk and learn how to stand out instead of blending in or following the script others had for me. I had to come to the end of my goals, my reputation, and my timelines and accept the invitation to be fully exposed before a perfect God. It meant casting away my formulas and my focus on just "trying harder." It meant coming out of hiding. The more I offered Him my flaws, my aching desires, and my scars, the deeper He brought me into His love for me. And as I had no choice but to loosen my grip, His peace and security began to flow and cover me.

This journey of discovery and release has not been easy, but it has brought me many realizations about myself, the titles I have chosen . . . and those that have been chosen for me. I realize now that I am unique and won't always fit in. But I strive to be true to myself—even when I am called to put on the "pastor's wife's face." A big part of my job is to share my husband with others as he pours himself into building the church body. But as a pastor's wife, there are times when I must guard myself and my family. Though you may not be aware of this, many people place expectations on us, often without realizing it, while the enemy whispers lies and tries to destroy us, our marriages, and our families. Despite the cost of the ministry calling, we are still human and experience real loneliness, jealousy, and temptation.

The question we must ask ourselves is this: *Who* am I, apart from my title? The list below includes real struggles and confessions shared by a diverse group of pastor's wives and women in ministry positions. I hope some of these resonate with you and help you feel seen and understood.

More Than Her *Who*:

- She listens, serves, leads, and prays.
- She longs for deep friendships inside the church, where she can be herself and feel invited and accepted.
- She may be judged unfairly or put on a pedestal with expectations.
- She appears confident in herself but is simply walking in faith, just like everyone else.
- She wants to hide or be anonymous.
- She gets angry or hurt by what is said about her husband as he gives his all to lead the church.
- She may have children who are not following Jesus and who may not want to come to church.
- Her heart aches with the struggles she is facing in her marriage while being called upon to be an example of a great marriage and pour into others.

For the beloved community of friends who surround those of us who hold titles, both in and outside of the church, we need you. You are answers to prayer, as you see us for who we are and not for the roles we have. You offer us the opportunity to let go of the part of us that represents the church and just be ourselves without any filters or explanations; it is truly sacred. And those sisters of mine who have given me a seat at the table just to be me; I may not always know how to answer the questions about how I am doing, but when you invite me to coffee or to share a hobby or simply offer to pray, know that it matters . . . know that it makes a difference.

In the Storm

Several years ago, I was in the throws of walking through some really hard seasons of church life. Our church leadership was experiencing major shifts, our congregation was changing, and many were leaving. And as if this wasn't hard enough, our church building was leveled by a tornado. After the tornado, we focused on praising God for His great mercy. No one was hurt or killed in that storm, and the direct hit to the church actually shielded houses and people nearby. With our building now unusable, my husband was placed as the leader in charge. He had more on him than one person should have to handle alone. I tried everything I could to support and lighten his load while continuing to pray and stay grounded in hope and expectation.

During that season, parenting our three sons well and navigating their unique needs was a full-time job. Our oldest, being on the Autism spectrum and entering teen years, was especially challenging. I often felt like I was failing at my first ministry roles as a wife and mother. Together, my husband and I were helping others—ministering, leading, and giving all we could.

One night, not long after the church had reopened and life was settling back in, I had a vivid dream. It was one of those super-fast dreams, but the kind you don't forget. In my dream, I remember someone grabbing my arm and asking me where all the bruises had come from. I quickly looked down and saw a number of purplish-yellow bruises covering my arms and legs. I had no idea where they had come from. After that short scene, I woke up.

As I began to wonder more about this dream and the bruising process, I realized those bruises were in the healing stages. Their yellowish color indicated they were not new but had been there for some time. After seeking wise counsel, I realized I, too, had been hit by the blows that struck our ministry. Even though they were not directed at me, I still faced them and felt their effects long after.

As I reflect on the different seasons of my life and my calling, I am drawn to the story of Queen Esther in the Old Testament. This beloved queen faced deep-seated obstacles and labels that disqualified her from the position God was calling her to. Based on her culture and the judgments made against her, she should not have been the one to fulfill such a high and prestigious calling. But God . . . He created her for a specific time and purpose, a purpose that would bring her to the end of herself and her capacity. Her uncle Mordecai, who adopted her, believed in her purpose and set before her a life-changing opportunity. It was a chance for her to abandon her unbeliefs and say *yes*—a chance to see herself as her uncle and God saw her. It was a chance to step into an appointed position and carry out her calling. Although it came with great risk to her own life and the lives of her people, she completed the assignment, believing all the while that her God went before her.

We are more like Esther than we know. God has placed us here at this time and for His purpose. This is **our** faith opportunity to humbly be His servant and choose to say, "Yes!"

The Invisible Tidal Wave

It's not a coincidence that most of our battles are fought in the invisible spaces that the human eye cannot see. The Bible speaks of spiritual battles we experience that are beyond the human lens. These battles can begin with a simple thought or situation we find ourselves in and then progress into feelings of anxiety, insecurity, or guilt. Pay attention to the thoughts, the situations, and, most importantly, the whispers that follow. They are curated to keep you from experiencing freedom from shame and the strongholds that block you from the goodness of God's promises and true community.

As a ministry leader, you can expect to face specific attacks in the areas where you are pouring into others. If you build up women to be strong and confident in their identity in Christ, you will be under more attack in this same area. The enemy knows just how to package up lies. And because you have kingdom influence and anointing over you, you are a threat, a dangerous threat. He knows that if you become healthy and whole inside and out, you will set others free, starting with their mindset and willingness to believe.

But remember, Jesus went first. He himself was tempted, ostracized, and ultimately killed for the very calling that was placed on His life. The enemy tried everything, but Jesus' weapon was choosing to be in connection with His Father while doing His Father's will.

You, too, are going to need a battle plan. What will be your weapons of warfare?

It requires regular Holy Spirit connection and training to combat this. Your defense is worship, prayer, and meditation over God's Word as you declare His Truth to prevail over darkness and sin. You will need a few others who you can trust will go to battle for you in prayer and spend time with you, providing counsel and wisdom. The greatest weapon will always be choosing not to fight alone.

Finally, in this journey, I had to give myself permission not to be the Proverbs 31 Woman. I am not her, and neither are you. Being in a church culture is a unique space. It can be the greatest gift, and it can also be the greatest disappointment. You will be praised and loved for who you are in some places. In other areas, you will experience judgment and criticism. Your job is not to change the culture. Instead, it is to be separate, leaning on the Spirit to fulfill you.

> **The greatest weapon will always be choosing not to fight alone.**

You are seen and connected to your husband's role in ways you did not sign up for. You have been given a strength and commitment to God's church that many don't have the capacity for. Your personality, passions, and perseverance are needed. Despite whatever success or failure is around you, who you are becoming will determine how whole and confident you become. This is not man's assignment but a God-sized dance you are being asked to join.

So stand strong, my sister, knowing **you** are the one God chose. Your life is a gift marked with beauty, strength, and purpose bigger than you could even begin to ask for or imagine. He wants you to thrive where He has placed you. But first, who is the woman you see in the mirror? Because of who He is within you, you bring kingdom value wherever you go before a word is ever spoken.

You are more than enough. You are more than a pastor's wife.

REFLECTIONS:

1. How is your role as a wife or a ministry leader tied to your identity or reputation?
2. What lies do you feel the enemy tells you? How can you lay those before God?
3. Who are the people that you can be absolutely and totally vulnerable with?

Sandra Coates is an author, speaker, fashion model, and coach committed to sharing her faith while empowering women of all ages to walk confidently in their identity and uniqueness. As the founder of a movement, UNITED + TRU, her team uses large fashion shows to showcase women and girls walking out their God story on the runway as role models. From food addiction to body shame, anxiety, and broken relationships, her passion is seeing every woman's beauty released as she shares her compelling testimony of how God invited her to leave her past and stop chasing after what she already had within her.

Sandra has faithfully served both in and out of the church in various positions, leading and mentoring countless women and girls to believe what God says about them and to live with the freedom and confidence He offers.

She also loves surfing and adventures with friends. Sandra is married to Brett, an executive pastor, and together they have three sons.

"Mary stood crying outside the tomb. While she was still crying, she bent over and looked in the tomb and saw two angels there dressed in white, sitting where the body of Jesus had been, one at the head and the other at the feet. 'Woman, why are you crying?' they asked her. She answered, 'They have taken my Lord away, and I do not know where they have put him.' Then she turned around and saw Jesus standing there, but she did not know that it was Jesus. 'Woman, why are you crying?' Jesus asked her. 'Who is it that you are looking for?' She thought he was the gardener, so she said to him, 'If you took him away, sir, tell me where you have put him, and I will go and get him.' Jesus said to her, 'Mary!' She turned toward him and said in Hebrew, 'Rabboni!'" [This means "Teacher."]

~John 20:11–16, GNT

CHAPTER 14

Meanwhile . . . But God

By Crystal Hall

Born a preacher's kid in 1973, I chose Christ at age four, and my baptism followed not long after. By age twelve, however, my parents divorced. This went against all I understood about the Bible. Though I had a new stepmother and stepfather, whom I loved dearly, the sting of God not answering my prayers for a restored family was held in bitterness. The Lord continued to chase after my heart, but I would not fully surrender. I could no longer see God's goodness through my anger, and I ran from His will for me, placing Him on a shelf and living for myself.

In my late teens and early twenties, I worked two jobs, went to night school, and lived with my family. During this time, a friend spent months trying to set me up on a blind date. I finally gave in with one condition— we had to talk first. That call lasted 3½ hours, and days later, I had a double date with a complete stranger. At the end of that evening, he walked me to my door, kissed me on the cheek, and left. Once inside, I began to cry. My mama, waiting in the kitchen, was startled by my tears and asked me what was wrong. I confessed, "I just met the man I am supposed to marry, but I'm not ready!"

Joey, the man I know God placed in my life, became the one I spent hours on the phone with every weekend and drove hours to see as often as possible. All I had ever desired as a little girl was to grow up to be a wife and mother, and those desires appeared to be coming true. Both shy of twenty-two, a year after our first date, we were married. I cannot describe how God blessed me with such a man. He filled all my gaps, shortcomings, and weaknesses. Though I had always been extremely high-strung, Joey was calm, selfless, soft-spoken, and loving. He was the wisest, kindest, humblest, and gentlest human I had ever known.

Time seemed to fly by, and Joey graduated from college after a year and a half of marriage. At that time, we had not been attending church. But due to some difficult circumstances and the loss of Joey's best friend to suicide, we felt God drawing us to Him. We soon found a church home and committed ourselves to following the Lord first and foremost.

Our son, Wyatt, was born after five years of marriage. I was working then, but Joey and I felt God was leading me to be a stay-at-home mom, and we obeyed. Our daughter, Millie, was born twenty months later. After almost a year at his new job and Wyatt approaching his 4th birthday, Joey and I believed the Lord was calling us to his hometown, hours away from my family, closer to his. Prayers were answered, and doors opened. We were in our new home within two weeks and soon began serving at a local church.

Before moving, my daddy became very ill with complications from diabetes, and after his passing, I felt as if my heart had been ripped out. Overwhelmed, I could not get past the grief of losing a parent. Joey walked me through the heartache, remaining patient while I found my way back from the depths. Throughout his illness, my daddy spoke about his pain and how his walk with the Lord had grown stronger. We talked about Paul's wrestling with the Lord, and he often referred to 2 Corinthians 12:8–10. He shared that he did not regret the suffering this disease caused him because it had brought him closer to the Lord. It would not be until later that I would fully understand and draw upon the truth of what my daddy had shared with me.

As Joey and I continued to grow in our faith, I knew God was calling me to serve Him in an unlikely way. Joey and I prayed for discernment and clarity. I believed God wanted us to have another child, and Joey (who had initially wanted six kids) emphatically told me to pray more. We both heard the calling two months later, and God blessed us with another baby girl a year later.

Joey and I were living life, serving our church, and watching our children thrive during this time. When our church started discipleship groups, we both became involved. Those groups were timely and life-changing for us, a safe place for accountability and digging deeper into the Word and the fellowship. It was then that the Lord threw us a curveball, moving us further out of complacency—calling us into fostering to adopt.

After much prayer together, we were sure of the direction in which God was leading us. Our family of five would become a family of seven. We adopted two wonderful boys, Collin and Cayson. It was a long, challenging, tearful, joyful, frustrating, and blessed journey. Throughout this four-year process, God continued to bless and multiply my prayer from years before—to be a mom. It was a learning curve, an enormous adjustment, and it still is. Through it all, God was and continues to be ever faithful. But that is a story for another day.

Just as we were beginning our foster journey, I began having many health issues. Chronic pain became a constant companion, and the treatments for each new issue caused me to be restricted to our couch. We eventually found a doctor who diagnosed what likely had been the leading cause of all my other health problems. I had Ehlers-Danlos syndrome, a connective tissue, and joint hyper-mobility disorder. The explanation for my kids was that I was Elastigirl, but I did not snap all the way back into place. It was also discovered that my knees did not sit in the normal position, a genetic issue. We were blessed to find the right doctors and begin the proper care, but I had to learn to ask for and accept help often. Asking for help had always been difficult because I did not want to inconvenience others. Joey's perspective was that of being prideful and selfish when I did not ask for help. Little did I know that those words would come back to me at a later date.

On December 26, 2021, my family was in church. No longer being back-row Baptists, Joey had moved our family to the front of the church a few months prior. As a member of the praise team, my view was of the congregation, but I typically worshiped with my eyes closed and hands raised. That morning, I only remember singing one song—"We Are So Blessed" by Bill and Gloria Gaither. As I sang, I felt the Holy Spirit nudging me to open my eyes. Oh, what a sight to behold! My husband was worshiping with his hands in the air, something he had never done before. I could not stop the tears from flowing. What a gift God gave me in that view. It was a memory to treasure, a special moment for our pastor and me . . . one that would be discussed in the days that followed.

Later that day, Joey and I drove along many of the old back roads we had traveled while dating. We reminisced, laughed a lot, and just enjoyed our alone time. Joey complained of severe heartburn after picking up one of our boys from basketball practice, but he said he was okay. After taking a few antacids, he went to bed. My daughter Millie, her friend, and I sat up talking about our upcoming mission trip. When I finally headed to bed, Joey took more antacids and confirmed again that he was fine.

Rising to my 6:00 a.m. alarm, it was unusual to find Joey still sleeping. He was always up before everyone else. I didn't wake him, knowing he had a restless night. But as I was preparing to leave with the girls, I became concerned and returned to our bedroom . . . and that is when my nightmare began.

I called 911, began CPR, and yelled for Millie and Wyatt, giving them a few instructions on whom to call. Our pastor arrived soon after, as did the EMTs. Little did I know, the yard would soon be filled with the cars of our friends and church family who had come to our aid. As we followed the ambulance, my heart was full of both dread and hope . . . not yet knowing that my life and the lives of my children were about to be shattered.

He had passed peacefully in his sleep. I lost the love of my life that day, the man God had so generously gifted me with. My children lost their adoring father. Although some of that day is a blur, much is etched clearly in my mind. As we exited the hospital doors, God gave us a sight to draw hope from—my church family, a sea of faces to support and grieve with us. I asked our worship leader to lead us in the song we sang just the day before—the day I witnessed my husband freely worshiping. The sweet melody of "We Are So Blessed" filled the air. I was so overcome with the sound that I could barely stand, yet the women gathered around me, supporting me and helping to keep my hands raised in praise! God had given me Aarons and Hurs!

Grief is hard. Actually, I don't believe words are descriptive enough to convey the emotions, pain, and heartbreak. It is a roller coaster, crashing waves, and sometimes a tsunami . . . a vicious cycle. Even after losing Joey, it seemed as though I was never allowed the time to sit with my grief—having lost my stepdad, two uncles, an aunt, and a grandmother since Joey's passing.

> **I don't believe words are descriptive enough to convey the emotions, pain, and heartbreak.**

During and after the funeral, our family was surrounded by our church family and friends in the community. As much heartache as I was feeling, I also had much joy and thankfulness that my children and I were experiencing the hands and feet of Jesus firsthand. Joey's funeral was an amazing worship service, a celebration of his life and God's goodness. "Promises" by Maverick City, "Goodness of God" by Bethel Music, "Gratitude" by Brandon Lake, and "We Are So Blessed" by Bill and Gloria Gaither were all sung at the service. How could I not stand, raise my hands, praising and thanking the Lord for the love and life He blessed me with in Joey? I remember many details of that day, little treasures God gave me to draw upon when the days ahead would grow dark. His presence overwhelmed me and comforted my soul.

In the days following the funeral, reality began to set in. Feeling like I had been ripped in half; days seemed like a nightmare, while nights were terrifying and lonely. Some moments were unbearable. Two years prior to his death, Joey had begun working from home. We saw each other much more, enjoyed lunches, and had day dates every other Friday. The longing and misery of missing his presence was now a reality I had never expected. We had dreams, the anticipation of later years, and the hopes for how

God would use and send us. I praised my Savior through it all, but it did not negate that I was agonizingly missing half of whom God had joined us to be.

Questions flowed through my mind . . . the whys, what-ifs, and hows. I even pondered what I could have done differently to change the outcome. Between grief and depression, severe anxiety, and ADHD, I felt like a chaotic mess. I began talking with a Christian counselor . . . one I know God led me directly to. How could I fill the role of a dad when I was never created for that? He called me to be a wife and mother, so who was I supposed to be when the title of "wife" no longer applies to me? I truly struggled with "me without the we."

Widow—I hated that word. It meant the love of my life was no longer here with me. For months, I wrestled with God about who I was and His plan for me now. I began to search through Scripture for everything I could find about widows. I read that He names us and calls for the care and protection of widows and orphans. James 1:27 says, "Religion that God our Father accepts as pure and faultless is this: to look after orphans and widows in their distress and to keep oneself from being polluted by the world." I read in Psalm 68:5 (ESV) that He is my defender. His Word says He is "father of the fatherless and protector of widows."

A dear friend, a widow herself, made a statement to me that I will never forget: "You are not a widow. You are a daughter of the King who happens to be a widow." My roles were skewed, and her words were God-given because they began to change the way I viewed myself. One of my closest friends also encouraged me to find the "good." Her words reminded me of the events in John 20:11–16. As Mary stood weeping outside the empty tomb, she did not realize she was experiencing a "meanwhile" moment. But just a few short verses later, Jesus stood before her—even in the waiting, in the meanwhile, God is still and always present.

Joey and I had planned to build an addition to our home when our fostering journey began. We needed the space for our boys to have an area for themselves, and It would also benefit me to be downstairs in a new master suite because of my health problems. Four years after we had begun designing the plans and three short weeks before his death, Joey talked with our good friend, who happened to be a contractor, about finally starting the addition. The delay had been caused by several factors: COVID-19, job security questions, and price increases. But it was time. After Joey's passing, our contractor and I had a conversation about what needed to be done. I decided the renovations were still needed because the boys required more room, and I still desired to be downstairs.

At the time of his passing, Joey was chairman of the deacons. He had a close relationship and bond with those men and our pastor. Joey's death hit many members of our church family hard, and the church deacons were definitely some of those. But what happened next truly amazed me. Never in my life have I felt so humbled as when this group of men met to discuss our home addition as that year's mission project. Men and women from the church showed up to build, paint, and clean our new addition while providing lunch and drinks during the long, hot days. We gathered for prayer each morning, and I cannot help but tear up when I think of their sacrifice of time, energy, and love for our family. What a complete picture! I was blessed to witness the hands and feet of Jesus, the body of Christ, and the church coming together to honor him! Scriptures were written on the doorposts, the flooring, and the walls—all hidden beneath the finished project. I will never stop praising the Lord for His goodness in my life and how He used so many to speak life back into my weary soul.

Listening to His voice, discerning His plan for my life . . . time spent waiting on the Lord is hard; the seasons of grief, mourning, and waiting have been painful. Though I was no longer a wife searching for my purpose, I needed time away from life's chaos—a beach trip. Heading out to my back deck before leaving, I noticed the neglect of my plants. Two fuchsias were in dire need of care. My favorite had hot pink and white blooms. The other was deep pink and purple. The purple one looked salvageable, so I watered what would hopefully survive and headed out.

Upon my return, I struggled to hold myself together. Grief engulfed me, depression had a grip on me, my anxiety was through the roof, and I had no understanding of what was happening. Pride aside, just as Joey had talked with me about, I knew that I needed to ask for help. I contacted a few willing and dear friends. Each was more than happy to help out, and many, thankfully, continue to do so. I began to breathe a little easier. Breathe . . . sometimes, I literally forgot to breathe. I got so caught up in who goes where and when and how I would manage it all while still trying to show up every day.

One Sunday afternoon, I needed sunshine and quiet for a few moments. I walked to the back deck, watered the recovering plants, and reached for the barren fuchsia. As I grabbed the handle of the hanging basket, the Holy Spirit clearly told me to sit. I did, contemplating the plant I wanted to discard.

As I sat there, I compared that plant to my life. The more I stared, the more I began to notice splashes of fresh, bright green hidden beneath the under-watered, overexposed leaves. My heart skipped a beat; life was still in this neglected plant. I started removing the crispy, withered leaves, and when I finished, it was stripped down to the stems, bare and exposed. But the bright green buds brought a glimmer of hope that the plant would survive.

God spoke to Moses in the burning bush. That day, He spoke to me in the image of a fuchsia plant. It's been hard finding the good in missing my godly leader, humble companion, encourager, calm to my chaos, provider, comforter, comic relief, partner in all things, and the other half of myself. But I keep trying. Pruning. Plants must thrive and flourish. In John

In the bearing of fruit, God is glorified.

15:1–8, Jesus tells us it is necessary for our lives if we are His children. We must remain in Him if we are to bear fruit. Sometimes, pruning happens to bear more fruit. In the bearing of fruit, God is glorified.

Pruning—the representation in a plant of what God was doing in my life. I once proclaimed how I depended on the Lord, but until Joey was no longer by my side, I had no idea how much I depended on my husband. His passing caused me to question who I depended on more. Joey was my earthly provider, partner, protector, love, and champion. Was God more so? My crisis of faith—did I truly trust God to be these things and more for me? Enough—did I truly believe He was and is enough? Everything belongs to Him, including my Joey. And although He blessed me with a treasure in my husband, God never promised us a definitive timeline. All of time is in His hands, including mine and yours. Since Joey's passing, I have spent much time in prayer reevaluating my walk with the Lord. I want Him to be my everything, my *enough*, which includes loving Him more than what He calls me to do in this life.

I am more than a wife, more than my dreams fulfilled. I am His redeemed, forgiven, sanctified child. In Ephesians 5:22–33, the Bible tells us the church is His bride. I am His bride—I am still a bride! And Revelation 19:7 says, "Let us rejoice and be glad and give him glory! For the wedding of the Lamb has come, and his bride has made herself ready."

He is my salvation, my song, and the One to whom I long to give glory and praise. I am a constant work in progress—still grieving and mourning—and I will be until He returns or calls me home. But in my time left on this earth, I want to be changed. I want to be more like Him. Even in the waiting . . . there's always a meanwhile. And in the meanwhile, God is continually present. Just as Paul proclaimed in Acts 20:24 (ESV), "But I do not account my life of any value nor as precious to myself, if only I may finish my course and the ministry that I received from the Lord Jesus, to testify to the gospel of the grace of God"—I pray I live as such.

I am more than a wife. I am His.

REFLECTIONS:

1. Do you trust God is working, even in the meanwhiles?
2. Do you live to honor Him in your calling, or does pride hinder total surrender to Him?
3. What is your "more than?" What do you need to lay at His feet and trust Him with today?

Crystal Hall is a mother to five wonderful children. She has been blessed to be a stay-at-home mom since her firstborn arrived. She is a recent widow, discovering daily what it means to truly and wholly rely on God. She is a Jesus follower, trying to live abiding in His presence and following Him in obedience. She loves to serve in missions, local and foreign. She is blessed to sing with the praise team, worshiping, and fellowshipping in her local church home. Her favorite place is sitting on her back porch with the logs on and a cup of coffee in hand. She enjoys reading, writing, drawing, hiking, and kayaking. She resides in northeastern Alabama with her family and their mini labradoodle, Blue.

"An excellent wife who can find?
She is far more precious than jewels."

~Proverbs 31:10, ESV

CHAPTER 15

Living Excellently

By Stefani Pady

(Hi friend, I want you to get the most out of the following few pages. Please take a moment to read Proverbs 31:10–31 so that the scripture is fresh in your mind.)

An excellent wife is something I have always dreamed of being, but it often feels impossible. Can you relate? Verse 10 of Proverbs 31 begins with a detailed description of the Proverbs 31 Woman and her noble characteristics. Many scholars believe it was advice from a momma (Bathsheba) recorded by her son (Soloman).

Even though King Solomon lived waaaaaaay back in the 900s BC, I am in awe at how much of Proverbs 31 (and the entire Bible) is still relevant today. But relevant or not, the Proverbs 31 Woman and her attributes seem daunting. Maybe striving to be this excellent woman causes you anxiety. Or maybe you don't even attempt to try because, let's face it, the Proverbs 31 Woman appears superhuman.

If Wonder Woman hailed from the Bible, this would be her bio.

If Wonder Woman hailed from the Bible, this would be her bio. Couple this with the fact that you may not be a wife in the first place, and this passage may feel like you are set up for failure before you even get to the second word in this verse—*excellent.*

179

In my younger years, my dreams of being a picture-perfect wife included visions of myself creating candle-lit date nights, making babies, and whipping up gourmet meals from scratch in my clean, fabulous kitchen. I daydreamed that my very own Prince Charming would sneak up behind me with kisses and roses. But deep in my soul, I always wondered if I would ever become a wife. Could anyone ever really love *me* . . . forever?

"She dresses herself with strength and makes her arms strong."
~Proverbs 31:17, ESV

As a young woman, my identity was interlaced with insecurity. I put up a facade of a strong, confident woman, but inside, I had an extremely broken self-image, especially related to my physical features. I find it interesting that out of twenty-one verses on the Proverbs 31 Woman, only one mentions a physical description. And of all available body parts, the one an excellent wife is said to have is strong appendages. This is not the feature I imagine men drooling over (even with all my insecurities, *arms* weren't the body parts I worried about). However, the older I get, the more I understand the value our arms have in loving others well and creating a life we love.

Proverbs 31 also mentions hands seven times. Our hands yield fruit, make bed coverings, give generously, earn income, and produce joy for our people. It saddens me to think about how much worth I placed on appearances (of myself and others) when the magic was literally at my fingertips. Instead of creating a space filled with the blessings my hands could produce for those in my reach, I obsessed over the bump in my nose, my oversized thighs, short legs, and even the blonde eyelashes I was born with. Yes, even my eyelashes fell short. How ridiculous is that?

Unfortunately, as a woman, I bet you understand. Self-doubt is often built into our DNA. Before I was ten years old, my mom was already dousing my blonde eyelashes with mascara. I remember her telling me stories about how, back in her day, she would use pliers to zip up her bell-bottomed jeans. Whether she intended to or not, she taught me that tight meant beautiful and makeup could hide deficiencies. "Beauty is painful," she would say. It would be many years before I learned what God had to say about beauty.

"Charm is deceitful, and beauty is vain, but a woman who fears the Lord is to be praised."
~Proverbs 31:30, ESV

Now, as a momma myself, I'm committed to helping my daughter eradicate self-destructive beliefs like this. I want to eliminate these damaging beliefs from your mind, too. We often don't realize the impact these negative thoughts have on our daily decisions. And these choices, good or bad, affect our future.

To hide my low self-image, I threw myself into work, grades, production, and perfection. Whether at the gym, in the workbook, or at the workplace, I was striving. I felt the need to generate my worthiness and was willing to work as hard as I needed to accomplish it. I compensated for the physical features I thought were flawed by achieving as many tasks as possible (with excellence).

Fast forward to a few years into life after college . . . I married a tall, dark, and handsome specimen of a man and loved every single bit of him. I relished in the image of our relationship and was giddy at the fact that somehow, by the grace of God, he chose *me*. I was committed to being a biblical, awe-inspiring picture of perfection for my husband. I saw the Proverbs 31 Woman executing flawlessly on a list of tasks, and I was up for the challenge. But it didn't take long for the dream of date nights, roses, and make-out sessions to be replaced with the reality of microwave pizza, arguments, clutter, stress, work emergencies, and dirty countertops. This "excellent wife" thing was for the birds. . . .

"The heart of her husband trusts in her, and he will have no lack of gain."
~Proverbs 31:11, ESV

I shared a bit of my story, but what's yours? Maybe you have never been married. Perhaps you met Prince Charming, but he turned out to be a frog. Maybe you are divorced, widowed, or just feeling less than excellent. If that is the case, and you have stuck with me this far, I am so proud of you. You don't need to be a wife to be excellent!

The Proverbs 31 Woman didn't become a superwoman when she married. She was already worthy and just happened to become a wife as well. No matter where you find yourself today, I hope to reframe your perspective of this elusive woman and yourself so that you can clearly understand how God sees women in all of our excellencies! Jesus said, "The truth will set you free" (John 8:32, ESV). Let's journey into biblical truth. We will meet real women in Scripture who were praised and deepen our understanding of our freedom in Christ.

Am I Excellent?

Take a moment to define the word *excellent* in your mind. Now, imagine an adorable five-year-old girl looking right at you. Maybe she is your daughter, your niece, or your favorite student in school. She's sporting a messy ponytail, chocolate milk around her mouth, and a big red pizza stain on her shirt. She looks at you squarely in the eyes and asks, "Am I excellent?" Would she need to be flawless for you to answer yes? Of course not! That bright-eyed little beauty doesn't need to be perfect to be excellent; she needs only to be her fearfully and wonderfully made self (Psalm 139). The same goes for you, my friend.

> *"And now, my daughter, do not fear. I will do for you all that you ask,*
> *for all my fellow townsmen know that you are a worthy woman."*
> **~Ruth 3:11, ESV**

The word *excellent* used in our anchor verse, Proverbs 31:10, is the same word Boaz used to describe Ruth as worthy in Ruth 3:11. This Hebrew word *hayil* is used throughout Scripture to mean courageous, determined, strong, powerful, mighty, and able. It is the same word used to describe David (1 Samuel 16:28) and to refer to mighty armies. A mighty army unites its soldiers, withstands attacks, adapts during setbacks, implements good strategy, welcomes innovation, and forges exceptional leadership. But like Ruth and David and His mighty armies, God didn't design us to be flawless but to be strong. And He chose to use *hayil* to describe a woman—how awesome is that?!

God's Word is chock-full of astonishing women. Women like Ruth (Ruth 1), Abigail (1 Samuel 25), Deborah (Judges 4), and Shiphrah and Puah (Exodus 1) are some of my favorite women in Scripture because they exude strength. These ladies weren't perfect. Most of them lived in seasons of oppression, sadness, and loneliness. They were widowed, single, married, homemakers, leaders, and caretakers, yet they were also courageous, determined, strong, powerful, mighty, able, and, dare I say, excellent!

Abigail: Strength and Snacks

(I encourage you to read all of 1 Samuel 25. You will see so many traits of the Proverbs 31 Woman in Abigail!)

> *"Now the name of the man was Nabal, and the name of his wife Abigail. The woman was discerning and beautiful, but the man was harsh and badly behaved; he was a Calebite."*
> **~1 Samuel 25:3, ESV**

If you haven't met Abigail before, you aren't alone. She's rarely examined in your typical church service. Abigail was married to Nabal, a wealthy man Scripture describes as worthless (1 Samuel 25:17). When David needed food for his army, he asked Nabal for assistance. Nabal refused, even though David and his men had protected Nabal's shepherds. One servant who witnessed the exchange told Abigail, and she made haste to help in hopes of saving her family (1 Samuel 25:18).

> *"Then Abigail made haste and took two hundred loaves and two*
> *skins of wine and five sheep already prepared and five seahs of*
> *parched grain and a hundred clusters of raisins and two hundred*
> *cakes of figs and laid them on donkeys. And she said to her young*
> *men, 'Go on before me; behold, I come after you.' But she did not tell*
> *her husband, Nabal."*
> **~1 Samuel 25:18–19, ESV**

Her decision to intercede would save David from making a mistake that would have threatened his God-given destiny of becoming Israel's king. If David had murdered Nabal, King Saul, the reigning king of Israel at that time, would have had a legitimate reason to hunt David down and kill him (which, incidentally, he was already trying to do without just cause).

God used Abigail to save David and protect the bloodline of our Savior, Jesus (who is one of David's descendants). Many of us skip over the "boring" pages of genealogy in the Bible, but these lists often tell an important story.

> *"She rises while it is yet night and provides food for her household*
> *and portions for her maidens."*
> **~Proverbs 31:15, ESV**

As I read about Abigail preparing to confront David, I can't help but think of the smorgasbord of refreshments she was ready to provide. It reminds me of how fortunate I am to live next door to my sister. When rain shows up on the forecast, she is the person who is headed straight to the super-sized stores to stock up on toilet paper, water, and canned goods. The next time a hurricane swoops into town (I live in Houston, Texas, and this happens with alarming frequency), I will be prancing my family next door because I know she is prepared.

"She opens her mouth with wisdom, and the teaching of kindness is
on her tongue."
~Proverbs 31:26, ESV

Our friend "Abby" was prepared. But this doesn't happen in a vacuum. She had help from a team of servants who trusted her wisdom enough to share vital information. One of these servants risked his life to expose the truth, and he trusted her to act with wisdom and kindness, not with folly (like Nabal).

Here is something to consider as we're exploring Abigail's story: Do you provide a safe space for your team and loved ones to share vulnerably? One of the promises I make when working with new clients is to demonstrate professional authenticity. It's hard to work with me and not be reminded that we will operate in reality together. When we allow our loved ones to have a safe space to speak truth, we build trust. Just as you and I don't like fitting into a box someone else created for us, your kids, friends, and colleagues shouldn't have to either.

"And David said to Abigail, 'Blessed be the Lord, the God of Israel,
who sent you this day to meet me! Blessed be your discretion, and
blessed be you, who have kept me this day from bloodguilt and from
working salvation with my own hand!'"
~1 Samuel 25:32–33, ESV

How beautiful is it that Abigail's team knew they could go to her with the facts? I expect she had previously proved her ability to assess situations and make sound decisions. This established trust. Just as the Proverbs 31 Woman considered a field and bought it, Abby went against the grain and acted confidently and with discernment.

Being fair and decisive is a strength we women hold, both in the

Being fair and decisive is a strength we women hold, both in the workforce and in our homes.

workforce and in our homes. We need not worry about appearances but must allow wisdom and kindness to flow from us in any situation. Note that kindness is not a weakness. Abigail's calculated steps were wise and bold. She displayed strength and gentleness while taking a risk.

> *"In the fear of the Lord, one has strong confidence, and his children will have a refuge. The fear of the Lord is a fountain of life, that one may turn away from the snares of death."*
> **~Proverbs 14:26–27, ESV**

Abby wasn't alone in her strength. We meet many other brave women in Scripture go against the grain and take risks. Shiphrah and Puah were Hebrew midwife overseers when the Israelites were enslaved in Egypt. When Pharaoh ordered them to murder all the newborn Hebrew boys, they refused to obey at great personal risk (Exodus 1). They feared God above Pharaoh, and He blessed them for it.

Deborah worked outside the home and was a judge and prophetess. Men looked to her for guidance and wisdom. Just like the Proverbs 31 Woman, Deborah was strong and able. In Judges 4, she confidently went into battle with Israel's military commander, Barak. Her trust in the Lord was so complete that she said, "Nevertheless, the road on which you are going will not lead to your glory, for the Lord will sell Sisera into the hand of a woman" (Judges 4:9, ESV). Talk about girl power!

Know Your Worth (And Where It Comes From)

> *"Do you not know that you are God's temple and that God's Spirit dwells in you?"*
> **~1 Corinthians 3:16, ESV**

I spent the better part of my life judging my "worthiness" by my ability to check boxes. I set out to accomplish more tasks (better than others) to be considered an excellent mom, wife, employee, sister, and daughter. If there was a title, I wanted it, and I wanted to be excellent at it.

It took me years to understand that as a believer in Jesus, the Holy Spirit dwells in me. He helps me make decisions, show generosity, achieve the unimaginable, and become more like Jesus—all for His glory. I had been missing a very important truth: I didn't need to comply with what other humans expected of me. Instead, I could let God captain my ship.

"Then the Lord God said, 'It is not good that the man should be alone; I will make him a helper fit for him.'"
~Genesis 2:18, ESV

Abigail, Deborah, Shiphrah, and Puah took risks and went against societal expectations to do the right thing. Similarly, today, we must fight the urge to give into society's, the church's, or even our own personal expectations when they don't match God's unique call for our lives. We were created to be "helpers" who can close a gap in the lives of our people, yes, *our* people, the ones we love most. . . . God created us to serve and help them in ways they cannot do on their own. Don't underestimate the importance of this. (See this chapter's resources for a podcast exploring the word *helper*, as it is used in the verse above, that will change your life.)

As a wife, when my vision of gourmet meals changed to frozen pizza and the candle-lit evenings turned into messy countertops, I lost sight of who I was meant to be. I thought the foundation of my worth lay with the titles I carried and the tasks I could check off. I strived relentlessly for perfection, submission, and other standards that God did not place on my life.

"The fear of the Lord leads to life, and whoever has it rests satisfied; he will not be visited by harm."
~Proverbs 19:23, ESV

However, when I leaned into my relationship with God, I began to perceive my value differently. I could laugh at the days to come (Proverbs 31:25). This joyfulness was more profound and deeper than simply feeling happy. It was and continues to be based on the confidence that I will be in God's hands even if things do not go my way. (Proverbs 14:26–27). Worry and fear were replaced with the unrelenting desire to know God more and place my trust in Him. The fear of not measuring up faded into resting in His plans, not mine.

> *"For whoever has entered God's rest has also rested from his works as God did from his."*
> **~Hebrews 4:10, ESV**

I once heard the word *rest* defined as a restorative break from labor and worldly striving. Hebrews 4:11 begins by encouraging us to strive to enter that rest. As you go about your day, I encourage you to strive. Strive with all your heart for rest and to let the importance of titles fade. Strive to rest in the salvation of Christ. Strive to remember the truth of God until His truth is so interlaced in your soul you cannot tell where you end and where Christ begins. That, my friend, is living excellently.[2,3]

---

2   Pady, Stefani. "The Joy Thief: What Actually Makes a House a Home." Women, Worship,& Work. Accessed Jan. 24, 2024, https://womenworshipandwork.com/making-a-house-a-home/.

3   Harper, Lisa. "What God Says about Women. Lisa Harper's Back Porch Theology. July 18, 2022. Website. Accessmore. https://www.accessmore.com/episode/What-God-Says-About-Women.

REFLECTIONS:

1. Read Proverbs 31:10–31. What traits of the Proverbs 31 Woman do you think describe you?
2. How has your definition of "excellent" changed? Celebrate the ways you are already excellent, and make a plan and set goals to develop new traits in areas of your life where you'd like to improve.
3. Read Proverbs 16:3. What areas of your life are you holding on to that you need to hand over to God (for Him to do excellent work in you)? How does this change your perspective on achieving excellence?

Stefani Pady is the founder and coach behind Women, Worship, and Work. In the midst of incredible success in her "dream" corporate job, she was burnt out. After reading the Bible from cover to cover for the first time, God laid a series of truths and a calling on her heart that became the foundation for her ministry at Women, Worship, and Work. She is now a Maxwell Leadership Certified Coach and professional speaker and trainer. Much of her time is spent coaching professionals working for midsize to large organizations and assisting them in identifying and resolving their personal and business challenges. Stefani uses her experience to minister to women by walking them through real-world applications of biblical truths. By pairing Biblical teachings with real-life, she aims to help women find confidence, clarity, passion, and purpose in life.

Beauty Awaits from the inside-out and outside-in.

We will explore every detail of God's wondrous creation. Starting with YOU! This wellness retreat is an immersive experience intended to get you back to the basics (mind, body, and HOLY spirit) by heightening your senses to what matters most: your vertical alignment, so you can horizontally serve, share and SHINE! Bonus: it includes a missions element!

Contact: hello@tamraandress.com

let's find out your

PROFIT INDENITY

Reveal Your Passion and Spiritual Gifts
Connection to Start & Grow Your Business

TAKE THE QUIZ TODAY!

Have you ever wondered what your purpose is?

Or how you could use your gifting as an global messenger for God?

Or, perhaps, how your spiritual gifts are connected to your prosperity?

Or how your passion propels your profit?

F.I.T. in Faith Network Resource Hub!

IT'S TIME TO ACTIVATE YOUR *god dream*

The F.I.T. in Faith Network Resource Hub will serve as a growth tool for you as a Fierce Female ready to Fight The Good Fight.

SPEAK, WRITE, BUILD, TESTIFY

Count this app as your Aaron and Hurr on your fulfilling and sometimes hard days of blazing the trail of your purpose-driven calling.

- **SOUND BIBLICAL BUSINESS SUPPORT - COURSES & CONTENT**
- **TRAINING & IMPLEMENTATION TOOLS**
- **TEMPLATES**
- **QUICK START RESOURCES**
- **FINANCIAL TRAJECTORY PLANS & MODELS**
- **COMMUNITY CONNECTIONS - FOCUS GROUPS**
- **LIVE OFFICE HOURS MONTHLY WITH Q&A AND ON THE SPOT COACHING**

This is a podcast for the messengers!
The called ones.
The mobilized ones.
The ones on mission to turn their message into a movement.

This show was designed for Declaring Truth, Transforming Narratives & *Catalyzing Christians to Speak, Write, Build & Testify.*

SUBSCRIBE & LEAVE A REVIEW FOR A SHOUTOUT ON AIR!

This is a movement of empowered legacy building, chain breaking, pioneers, liberating others to stand in freedom, firm in their identity, and activating authority as Kingdom citizens. Join the movement today.

WE ARE THE MOBILIZED CHURCH!

ACKNOWLEDGMENTS

We take this present moment to acknowledge the stories that are shared on these pages. Some, for the very first time, have taken a leap of faith in bold courage to say yes to the journey of becoming a messenger. Letting the Lord who breathed life into them, breathe life through the words they are willing to release for another woman to find a fresh inhale and exhale in her dark, slow, sometimes lonely, breathless season. This project wasn't just meant for the reader, sis, it was meant for you too. Thank you for releasing your roar, so others can do the same. You are all fierce females. And I'm grateful to co-author a chain-breaking, legacy-leaving book with you. Special recognition to the heart-led developers of this book and concept. Janis Rodgers whose hearts' mission is to free women into their full identity and help them realize they are More Than a Mom; this book wouldn't exist without your seed planted. Candice Brown, for believing in the mission of F.I.T. in Faith Press and nurturing the stories of each of these authors so beautifully; your story is represented in every single page because YOU are more than enough in every category. Sharon Miles, our fearless editor, who is willing to take on the emotional weight of guiding first-time and seasoned writers through navigating their story in written format to share with the world. Finally, thank you to David Hancock and Morgan James, for your commitment to supporting the big vision of our Publishing House.

ABOUT THE AUTHOR

Tamra Andress is an international speaker, six-time #1 best-selling author, top 1 percent podcaster, and marketplace minister. Tamra's life journey, directly linked to leadership, entrepreneurship, and relationship, has gifted her the title of "entrepreneurial rabbi." Her quarter-life crisis led to an early-life catapult in her teaching, speaking, and serving career. She would have never imagined her greatest  weaknesses would become her greatest opportunities to help others lead a life of Truth and fulfillment at the intersection of faith and business. Her multiple best-selling books, top .3 percent podcasts, keynote speeches, events, publishing house, and non-profit are all based on the foundation of our rooted identity and intended catapult within our calling. She brings magnetic, joy-filled energy into every space, offering life and business principles that will break every stronghold and barricade blocking a life of true sustenance over success.

A free ebook edition
is available with the
purchase of this book.

To claim your free ebook edition:

1. Visit MorganJamesBOGO.com
2. Sign your name CLEARLY in the space
3. Complete the form and submit a photo of
   the entire copyright page
4. You or your friend can download the ebook
   to your preferred device

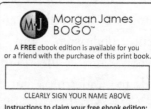

Print & Digital Together Forever.

Snap a photo

Free ebook

Read anywhere

Printed in the USA
CPSIA information can be obtained
at www.ICGtesting.com
JSHW020952100824
67891JS00005B/8

9 781636 984360